ESTATE PLANNING

FROM AVOIDING PROBATE AND ASSESSING ASSETS TO ESTABLISHING DIRECTIVES AND UNDERSTANDING TAXES, YOUR ESSENTIAL PRIMER TO ESTATE PLANNING

101

VICKI COOK and AMY BLACKLOCK

Founders of *Women Who Money*

Adams Media

New York   London   Toronto   Sydney   New Delhi

Adams Media
An Imprint of Simon & Schuster, Inc.
100 Technology Center Drive
Stoughton, Massachusetts 02072

First Adams Media hardcover edition August 2021

ADAMS MEDIA and colophon are trademarks of Simon & Schuster.

For information about special discounts for bulk purchases, please contact Simon & Schuster Special Sales at 1-866-506-1949 or business@simonandschuster.com.

The Simon & Schuster Speakers Bureau can bring authors to your live event. For more information or to book an event contact the Simon & Schuster Speakers Bureau at 1-866-248-3049 or visit our website at www.simonspeakers.com.

Manufactured in the United States of America

ISBN 978-1-5072-1639-2
ISBN 978-1-5072-1640-8 (ebook)

3 2023

Library of Congress Cataloging-in-Publication Data
Names: Cook, Vicki, author. | Blacklock, Amy, author.
Title: Estate planning 101 / Vicki Cook and Amy Blacklock, founders of Women Who Money.
Description: First Adams Media hardcover edition. | Stoughton, MA: Adams Media, an imprint of Simon & Schuster, Inc., 2021. | Series: Adams 101 | Includes index.
Identifiers: LCCN 2021013721 | ISBN 9781507216392 (hc) | ISBN 9781507216408 (ebook)
Subjects: LCSH: Estate planning--United States--Popular works. | LCGFT: Law for laypersons
Classification: LCC KF750.Z9 C664 2021 | DDC 332.024/0160973--dc23
LC record available at https://lccn.loc.gov/2021013721

CONTENTS

INTRODUCTION

Estate planning means different things to different people. For some, it may involve complex healthcare plans and extensive planning for distributing various types of property. For others with fewer assets, it may be simpler. But whatever your situation, estate planning is a necessary part of your life. Estate planning, at its simplest, means deciding what assets you have and what will happen to them when you pass on. It's a way of determining the kind of future you want to give your loved ones.

Estate Planning 101 will help you learn the ins and outs of this process. You'll know who's involved each step of the way, what decisions you must make, when to make changes, where you can store documents, and why particular circumstances may impact your planning. You'll also understand the importance of communicating your plan to others and how to go about doing so.

This book will help you create a safeguard for those you leave behind. By learning how to plan your estate, you'll be able to determine who gets your property and who'll be the guardian of your kids. Estate planning also protects you and your finances and safeguards your right to make decisions and control your assets during your lifetime and when you die. Essential estate planning paperwork includes a living will, financial and healthcare power of attorney documents, and a last will and testament. You may decide to complete certain forms on your own, or you may seek out the help of an estate planning attorney. Whatever you decide, the entries in this book will help guide you on the best path.

Additionally, *Estate Planning 101* will enable you to look beyond your estate and strategize for retirement, taxes, emergencies, end-of-life arrangements, and the legacy you want to leave behind. This book will help you determine if what you're doing today aligns with what you want your future to hold. By the time you finish, not only will you know the steps to take, but you'll also have the ability to reflect and clarify how your vision will impact your plans.

With this knowledge, you can take action and begin creating your estate planning documents. You may choose to start with just essential medical documents and a will and build the rest of your estate plan over time. Or you may be motivated to tackle the job now and develop a more comprehensive plan right away. Either way, you can use *Estate Planning 101* to help guide you in building a solid foundation for your estate. With it by your side, you will create a robust and complete estate planning path to help you and your loved ones secure your future.

Chapter 1

What Is an Estate, and Why Does It Require a Plan?

You may not consider what you own to be an estate. But as you read this chapter, we hope you'll realize estate planning should start when you're young, healthy, and beginning to accumulate money and valuable possessions. While your plan can evolve as you age, waiting to create one puts you, your family, and your assets at risk.

Chapter 1 introduces you to the estate planning process and provides an overview of several topics you'll learn more about throughout the book. In addition to the "ins and outs" of different documents, we also address the emotional side of making decisions. Estate planning is rarely easy, and it can be more challenging if you have complex assets or family dynamics. But it's worth all the effort. We think you'll feel that way too, once you consider your heirs and estate and how you want to protect them.

YOUR NEED FOR ESTATE PLANNING

Protecting Yourself, Loved Ones, and Valuables

When reading the word "estate," you may envision wealthy people with sprawling mansions, luxury cars, and millions in net worth. But when you own anything of value, you have an estate—and it's essential to have a plan in place for it after you pass on.

Considering your mortality is no easy task. But it's necessary to determine who'll make decisions for you if you're not able and how to divide your assets when you're no longer here.

You may think you won't deal with these issues until you start showing wrinkles. Yet the truth is, people get seriously ill or die in accidents every day, at any age.

Organizing estate planning is a smart move. While you can adopt habits promoting long and healthy living, planning for the worst is the best way to protect yourself, those you love, and your valuables.

WHAT MAKES AN ESTATE

Your estate comprises the assets you accumulate and hold at any one time. You may have a relatively small estate in your twenties and thirties, but it's likely to grow over the years.

Your house, cars, and bank or investment accounts are all part of your estate. Your assets also include retirement accounts, pension benefits, and cash-value life insurance. If you own a business, it's part of your estate too.

Everything you possess and value—including personal belongings—makes up the estate you'll pass on to heirs and favorite causes at your time of death.

PURPOSE OF AN ESTATE PLAN

Perhaps, if you've looked into estate planning, you've heard that one purpose of it is to minimize taxes and the fees of probate. But what is "probate"? Briefly, it is the legal process of reviewing a deceased's estate. Reduced taxes and fees are crucial aspects of estate planning, but there's more to it than just saving money and court time.

An estate plan gives you control over protecting your property and possessions and distributing them after your death so they support heirs and beneficiaries the way you want them to.

Your estate plan also protects you. If you become mentally or physically incapacitated, is there someone to manage your healthcare? What about your financial and legal affairs? Who's able to address estate matters when you die? You make those decisions during estate planning.

Legal Incapacitation

When suffering from incapacitation, you can no longer care for yourself, your property, or legal and financial matters. The court determines legal incapacity based on their judgment from medical evaluations and personal interviews. Depending on the cause, legal incapacitation may be temporary or permanent.

Estate plans protect your heirs too. In the planning process, you designate who receives which of your assets and when. If heirs are minors or otherwise immature or irresponsible, you can direct how they receive their benefits. An estate plan also helps your beneficiaries by protecting some of the assets from creditors, lawsuits, and bankruptcy.

Think of estate planning as a three-pronged approach to controlling your future. You're in control of your estate plan in the present. It protects you if an accident or illness takes away your ability to earn an income or manage your money. When you're no longer here, your plan controls the allocation of assets in your estate to heirs.

WHAT GOES INTO AN ESTATE PLAN

If you search "estate planning" online, you'll find lists of tasks to complete and templates to fill out. But keep in mind, your plan is unique to you and your situation. It allows you full control in deciding how your assets provide for you and your family and the legacy you leave behind.

Estate planning goals focus on:

- Providing financial security for you, a spouse/partner, and immediate family
- Naming a representative to handle financial and medical matters
- Financial support or gifts of personal property and possessions to others
- Funding a college education for children or grandchildren
- Minimizing expenses such as taxes, fees, and probate or administrative costs

- Avoiding disputes over your estate and final wishes
- Providing financial support to favorite charitable causes
- Transferring business ownership to a child, partner, or agent

During the process, you'll inventory your assets and liabilities. After considering future needs and those of your family, you'll decide how to address them best.

You'll choose between hiring an attorney or using templates or Internet-based DIY services to create your documents. You may decide setting up a trust makes sense for your estate. For small business owners, succession planning is a must.

Depending on your state of residence and your estate's size, consulting with an attorney or tax professional to find ways to minimize estate and inheritance taxes may be necessary.

These are the essential building blocks of most estate plans. For personal or financial reasons, you may be ready to attempt only some of the previous steps. Just know, the more you can tackle now, the better prepared you'll be. Estate planning isn't a one-time event either. You'll need to revisit your strategy as you grow older so it continues to align with your values and goals. Fortunately, once your fundamental plan is in place, making updates becomes more straightforward.

WHAT IF YOU FAIL TO PLAN?

When you can no longer make competent decisions or if you die suddenly without having an estate plan in place, the judicial system takes control. A court-appointed guardian makes decisions about your assets and healthcare. They also oversee asset distribution when you pass away.

There may be little left for heirs if you don't plan accordingly. Creditors can seek payments, and estate taxes and court fees may devour any nest egg you save. Rather than receiving money to support them, your family may need to sell valuable belongings to cover your final expenses.

Worst of all, due to state laws, someone can ignore your wishes about guardianship for your children, end-of-life care, or division of your possessions when you don't have a will. When you fail to plan, you're giving up your rights to make those decisions.

You Need an Estate Plan

You may be putting off estate planning because you think it's an expensive and emotional process. And it may be. But a little effort goes a long way, and paying some money now may help you save more later. To protect yourself and those you care about, the best time to start is today.

WHO TO CONSIDER IN YOUR PLANNING

Who You'll Protect, Trust, and Gift To

Everyone's estate plan is different. Individual needs vary depending on assets, family, goals, timelines, and more. But, as part of the planning process, we must determine who to protect, who we trust to carry out our final wishes, and who we want to receive our stuff.

IT STARTS WITH YOU

The first "who" to consider in estate planning is you. It's vital to protect yourself, your income, and your finances if a disability or incapacitation leaves you unable to make medical or financial decisions. Don't skip this because you're young or healthy. Accidents and unexpected illnesses can happen to us all.

To protect your income, you can buy disability insurance. You can be sure healthcare wishes are followed by preparing medical directives authorizing someone to act on your behalf when you cannot. Through a power of attorney (POA) document, you can appoint an agent to manage your finances. This brings us to the next "who."

WHO YOU'LL TRUST

It's time to consider who plays a legal role in your affairs if you become incapacitated or die unexpectedly. Your choice may be easy when you lead an uncomplicated life, have modest assets, and have close family relationships. But if your situation is more complex, it's necessary to balance emotions and the financial impact of decisions you make about guardianship, directives, trusts, and beneficiaries.

Designated Agent

Who do you trust to act as your designated agent in financial or medical situations when you cannot speak for yourself? It might be your spouse, sibling, child, another relative, or dear friend. While thinking over who's trustworthy enough to act on your behalf during your lifetime, you also need to identify who can carry out your wishes upon your death.

Executor or Personal Representative

An executor or personal representative is named in your will to handle your estate. After you die, this person manages your legal and financial affairs, including payment of debts and property distribution. Depending on your estate's size and complexities, this may be a time-consuming role that extends from managing funeral arrangements to your estate's legal closing. The chosen executor should be a responsible, patient, and financially stable individual you trust to carry out your final matters.

Guardian for Minor Children

When you have minor children, establishing who assumes their guardianship in the event of your passing is a must. While a surviving parent usually has custodial rights, a court generally appoints a close family member as guardian when there's no surviving parent or a valid will in place. This, however, may not be the person you'd choose to raise your children.

You'll want to think about who can provide the love and care your children will need. When possible, choose someone who has values closely aligned with yours, and make sure they're able and willing to accept guardianship in the event something happens to you.

Guardians for Dependents with Special Needs

If you have a child with special needs or have responsibility for a loved one with a disability, minor or not, executing a will and naming a guardian is imperative. Choose a willing individual who can best manage your loved one's emotional, physical, and fiscal care.

Since there are many roles loved ones can play in your estate plan, you may decide to name different people to fill those parts. Look at each individual's strengths and determine who could best handle taking on the additional responsibility of managing your care, the care of your children, and the distribution of your estate. Consider hiring a legal or financial firm to take on some of these responsibilities for you as well.

WHO YOU NEED OR
WANT TO CARE FOR

In addition to protecting yourself, your plan helps you provide support for loved ones. If married, you'll likely strategize as a couple. Looking after each other in addition to any minor children should be the primary goal. But there are others you may need or want to take into account during planning.

What to Think Through
Important considerations as you work on your estate plan:

- One another's dependency on your income or assets
- Someone's entitlement to your property through ownership rights
- Those you want to give your assets or personal possessions to
- If you want control over assets you leave behind
- Plans to disinherit anyone
- Relationship dynamics/interactions with your extended family members

Who to Consider
When reviewing the "who" in your planning, think about their immediate and future needs. For example, you may want to develop a plan to pay your children's or grandchildren's college expenses or detail what happens to assets if your spouse remarries after your death. Those people to consider include:

- Spouse or Partner
- Children/Stepchildren
- Grandchildren
- Parents
- Siblings
- Nieces/Nephews
- Other Relatives
- Pets

- Friends
- Business Partners
- Charities
- Ex-Spouses/Stepchildren

COMMUNICATING DESIRES AND DECISIONS

When it comes to estate planning, having conversations with family members is critical. Before drafting your plan, talk about how people feel regarding different details. Discuss if they have concerns about assuming guardianship of your children or accepting a power of attorney or personal representative position on your behalf. More conversations can occur once you finalize your estate plan.

You'll want to tell your immediate family and those you've designated to act on your behalf about the legal paperwork you've prepared. You don't have to go into detail about what's being distributed or to whom. They simply need to know you have a plan in place. You'll also want to share the documents' location and provide copies to your designated agents and representatives. Once done, you can feel confident you're protecting yourself and the people who matter most.

WHAT TO CONSIDER IN YOUR PLANNING

It's More Than What You Own

A significant part of estate planning involves managing and protecting assets so they provide for you and your immediate family during your lifetime and after your death. It also allows you to choose who receives your property and personal possessions when you pass away. Planning helps you define how you'll use assets in the short term while also growing and safeguarding them for retirement and future financial goals.

WHAT ARE YOU PROTECTING?

We've mentioned the words "protect" and "protecting" a lot. But you might be wondering what you even need to safeguard, so let's clear that up now. Estate planning includes not only tangible items but intangible things as well. It consists of what you have now, what you expect to have in the next few years, and what you're planning long term.

While we can't prepare for everything, we can plan a lot more effectively with some knowledge and awareness.

Your Income

Protecting one's income is often overlooked, but it's a critical move to maintain your financial health and the well-being of those you support.

Multiple Ways to Earn Income

You actively earn income when you receive payment in the form of wages, salary, tips, or commissions. Passive income comes from interest earned on savings accounts, rental-property activities, or a business venture in which you're not actively involved. Dividends, capital gains, and interest on investments are types of portfolio income.

As an employee, you may receive employer-paid benefits such as disability and life insurance coverage. But if you don't have these benefits or their value isn't enough to meet your needs, you can buy stand-alone policies from reputable companies.

Insurance policies are almost always cheaper to buy when you're young and healthy. So consider obtaining coverage for more than your current needs, especially when you're looking to grow your family or you expect your lifestyle to change.

Your Property

You'll take a deep dive into determining the nature and value of your estate in Chapter 2. But you can start preparing now by thinking about the real property and personal possessions you own.

There are two kinds of property: real property and personal property. We define real property as land and anything on it that's not easily moved, such as homes, barns, sheds, fences, bushes and trees, and water. Personal property in your estate, on the other hand, includes all the things you own that are moveable (that is, aren't real property): for example, the car you drive, belongings in your home, clothes, jewelry, art, and the cash in your wallet. Assets such as bank accounts, certificates of deposit (CDs), stocks and bonds, retirement and health savings accounts, life insurance policies, intellectual property and copyrights, and business ownership are all considered personal property.

Types of Real Property

Here are five types of real property investors use to build wealth:

1. **Agricultural:** farms, livestock ranches, orchards, timberland
2. **Residential:** single or multifamily, apartments, condos, master-planned communities
3. **Commercial:** offices, retail, hospitality, storage units, parking lots/structures
4. **Industrial:** factories, power stations, warehouses
5. **Mixed-use:** multiuse property, i.e., both residential and commercial

Your Relationships

Money—or, more accurately, the desire for it—can make people do strange things.

We hope your planning and situation remain free of conflict. Still, we'd be lax if we didn't mention the need to consider potential disputes when it comes to providing for and gifting assets to others.

Marriages and divorces, births and deaths, and career or entrepreneurial endeavors can change relationships and family dynamics. All of these events and more can potentially cause unforeseen disagreements.

You've likely heard stories of relationships destroyed due to perceived financial unfairness. Maybe you've even witnessed bitterness, friction, and questionable behaviors among relatives if you've already lost a grandparent, parent, or another family member.

Carefully consider who and what you're protecting. The "why" behind your intentions can help you create an estate plan that averts issues while providing the comfort and security you desire.

INSTRUMENTS FOR PROTECTION

There are various tools you can use to protect what's been mentioned previously. Next, we provide a brief introduction for several of these tools, but you'll read about them in more detail in later chapters.

- **Prenuptial Agreement (Prenup):** An agreement a couple creates before marriage, detailing what would happen to their assets and liabilities in the event of a divorce or the death of one spouse.
- **Postnuptial Agreement (Postnup):** A legal contract between an already married or civil union couple describing what would happen to their estate if the marriage were to end, through divorce or death.
- **Beneficiary Designation:** Naming of a person or entity (such as a charity) to receive the proceeds of a life insurance policy or financial instrument or the distributions from a will or trust.
- **Payable on Death (POD):** An arrangement between you and your bank or credit union naming a beneficiary to receive assets after you die.
- **Transfer on Death (TOD):** An arrangement similar to a POD but used to name a beneficiary on investment and retirement accounts.
- **Power of Attorney (POA) and Healthcare Directives:** Legal documents in which you designate another person(s) to act on

your behalf, to carry out or make financial or healthcare decisions in particular situations and matters.

- **Will:** A legal document detailing your assets' distribution to heirs and beneficiaries after your death.
- **Trusts:** A legal relationship in which you're designating another individual or institution (trustee) to certify and hold assets for particular beneficiaries until your passing or another time specified by you.
- **Insurance:** A purchased contract providing financial coverage or reimbursement for specific losses or expenses incurred.

As you can see, estate planning is not just for the wealthy. It involves much more than listing a beneficiary on a 401(k) at work or asking a sibling to take care of your child if you pass away unexpectedly.

We all need to do something if we want to protect ourselves and the people and things we care about.

MAKING YOUR DECISIONS

The Emotions and the Math

Once you determine who and what you need to protect, you can start making goals and essential decisions. The more carefully you plan, the less chaos loved ones will experience while mourning your death. With a plan in place, your family can avoid a lengthy and costly probate.

When going about the process, pay as much attention to your feelings as you do the figures. While splitting things equally or leaving assets in the most tax-efficient manner are worthy goals, there's no one formula that's right for everyone. Follow your heart when weighing gifting decisions and choosing heirs and representatives. After all, this is *your* estate plan.

ESTATE PLANNING GOALS

At this point, you may have a good idea of what you want from your estate plan. Take time to list your goals to make sure you don't miss anything (or anyone!) when you create your legal documents.

As you strategize, it's essential to be realistic. While you might want to pay for a child's college education, taking care of yourself and your spouse or partner first is the priority.

Make Your List

Following are some common goals to consider. Review the list and then create your own, keeping in mind that this one is not exhaustive and that all items may not apply to you.

- **Protect:** income, yourself in case of incapacitation, assets in case of divorce or litigation
- **Provide:** for self, spouse/partner, minor children, adult children with special needs, grandchildren, parents, siblings, or pets
- **Accumulate:** savings to pay for children's education, savings for retirement, or rental properties for cash flow
- **Name/Appoint:** beneficiaries, guardian for minor children, representative, and agents
- **Leave:** specific gifts or heirlooms to relatives or friends
- **Donate:** financial gifts to charitable, educational, or religious organizations
- **Maintain:** privacy, control of certain assets, generational legacy, and ownership of real property or businesses within family members
- **Avoid:** conflicts, hurt feelings, taxes, fees, and mistakes!

Planning Considerations

When leaving everything to a spouse and any children you have together, deciding who gets what may be simple. However, if you have children with another person, stepchildren, or immediate family members disgruntled with you or each other, the division of things can be challenging. How you handle distributing assets to these people should be done with care.

Potential Challenges

Begin thinking about unique circumstances you'll need to address in your plan. Examples include kids from prior relationships, relatives with special needs, adult children not speaking to you, property owned with your best friend, or a business inherited from Mom. You'll want to explore the best way to handle the transfer or gifting of assets in these situations.

You may also have a former spouse who feels entitled to an asset you shared in that marriage. There should be no issue if it's part of your legal divorce agreement. But when there's only a verbal agreement between the two of you, formally include this information in your estate plan.

Leaving Someone Out

Intentionally choosing not to leave property to an immediate family member or someone who expects to receive something after your death is called disinheritance.

In most states, disinheriting a spouse is not allowed due to common law. We cover those specifics in Chapter 7. But you can choose to disinherit a child or another member of your family—likely not an easy decision. Our best advice is to take your time and carefully weigh the pros and cons of choosing disinheritance against other options.

Leaving someone other than a child without any rights to your property may be as simple as not listing them in your will. However, if you choose to disinherit a child, you must specifically state so in your will. While no law requires an explanation for the disinheritance, you may provide a reason if you wish. Doing so may also prevent anyone from challenging your will later. A child you fail to disinherit by name, or a child accidentally omitted, may make a claim for a portion of your estate.

BENEFICIARY DECISIONS

Aside from choosing a guardian for minor children, establishing beneficiaries could be one of the hardest things you'll do. You have the right to decide who receives what from your estate, and you can disinherit anyone you choose. Including a note explaining why you opted to divide assets in a specific way may help avoid unintended hurt feelings or disagreements.

Beneficiaries named on insurance policies and financial accounts override what's written in a will. So, you must rename beneficiaries on those items whenever there's a change in circumstances. Life events such as marriages, divorces, births, adoptions, and deaths are likely times when updating beneficiaries is necessary.

Types of Beneficiaries

You can designate one primary beneficiary to receive specified property or name multiple primary beneficiaries by providing each with a specific amount or percentage of the asset. For example, you could leave 100 percent to your spouse, or 50 percent to your spouse and 25 percent to each of your two children. Contingent or alternate beneficiaries are listed to receive the named property in cases where the primary cannot. For example, if your spouse or partner is the primary beneficiary of your life insurance policy but you pass away together in an accident, the contingent or alternate beneficiaries named on the policy receive the payout instead.

A life estate beneficiary is someone to whom you leave the right to use a property without them becoming the legal owner of the property. You might do this when you want to allow a second spouse to remain in your home but want your child to inherit the property after your spouse's death. In this case, you're designating your child as the final beneficiary.

Minors

Minor children, those under the age of eighteen in most states, are not allowed to own assets over a specific value. They're also not allowed to enter into contracts or hold real property until reaching adult status. When you want to leave money or items for minors, you can give them to a parent or guardian to manage with the minor's best interests at heart. Gifting assets to the child and naming a custodian or property guardian to oversee them is also an option. You can find specifics on these decisions in Chapter 4 on wills and Chapter 5 on trusts.

Pets

Legally, pets cannot hold property. Leave pets and any money for their care with a relative or friend who agrees to the responsibility. You can also establish a trust and name a trustee to manage the money left for the maintenance of your pets.

PLANNING THROUGH LIFE STAGES

Life Isn't Static; Neither Is Your Plan

As emphasized earlier in this chapter, estate planning is a process to start when you're young, healthy, and accumulating assets. Even if you're statistically unlikely to get a severe illness or die at a young age, having a plan in place for your money and possessions spares loved ones more work in the event of a tragic situation.

Your estate plan evolves as goals, family, assets, and income levels change. The strategies and tools you use to achieve goals may change too. Legislation related to estate planning also evolves over the years and may impact your strategy. Your plan needs to reflect your current situation. Otherwise, beneficiaries may not be protected when your life comes to an end.

LIFE TRANSITIONS

Right now, you might be single with no children or coming up on your tenth wedding anniversary and the birth of a third child. No matter your circumstances, an estate plan can benefit you now. However, future needs and the needs of those who depend on you may require you to adjust your plan as time goes on.

While this section can't help predict the future, it provides awareness of what you may encounter at various times and life stages and when your plan may need adjustments.

Young and Solo

When single and childless, your estate planning needs are simple. They include a will, POAs, and advance healthcare directives with a Health Insurance Portability and Accountability Act (HIPAA) release. At this stage, you'll likely name a parent or sibling as beneficiary and representative of your estate. You must have these documents so your family can make decisions for you if you cannot.

Life and disability insurance may be provided through an employer, but if not, consider obtaining policies.

HIPAA

The HIPAA Privacy Rule limits who can view and receive your health information. Rules specify what can be used and shared so your information is protected while not interfering with your care. Learn more on the US Department of Health and Human Services website: www.hhs.gov/hipaa/for-individuals/guidance-materials-for-consumers/index.html.

Engagement and Marriage/Life Partnership

Before tying the knot, think through preparing a prenuptial agreement. Prenups are beneficial to couples entering a marriage with significant assets or large amounts of debt. Those who anticipate a high future income, a substantial inheritance themselves, six-figure student loans, or various other issues may also want a prenup. If you're already wed, a postnuptial agreement may be for you.

While no one likes to think their marriage could dissolve, almost half of all marital partnerships in the United States end in separation. Besides determining the division of assets and debts in a divorce, prenups can help you be more financially transparent with each other and assist in your financial planning.

Once you commit to a long-term relationship or say, "I do," you both need to take steps to protect each other.

Becoming a Parent/Stepparent

Once you have a child through birth or adoption or become a stepparent, naming a guardian for them is critical. You'll also want to evaluate your asset distribution plan and audit the financial protections you have in place.

Look at adding or increasing life and disability insurance policies as well. When you have more kids, a loss of your income could be more financially devastating. A few more dollars per month for thousands of dollars in increased coverage can bring peace of mind.

Divorce or Death of a Spouse or Heir

The loss of a spouse, partner, or child is devastating. As you pick up the pieces and move on in life, you'll also need to make adjustments to your plan. Who can assume the legal roles your spouse was designated to fill? Who do you leave your home and car to now? We know the answers may not come easily when you're grieving a loss, but you'll need to address your plan to ensure you and your estate are protected.

Remarriage

If you remarry, your estate planning documents and beneficiary accounts may need to reflect the change. What property are you sharing with your new spouse? How can you protect them while also protecting any children from prior relationships? You'll need to consider these types of questions and evaluate your plan for necessary updates.

Wealth Accumulation

No matter your marital status or age, as you accumulate assets and experience more life events, you likely need to update your estate plan.

You may opt to start a trust so assets can pass more quickly to your heirs without going through probate. The addition of a donor-advised fund could be an option to support favorite charities. Or you may want to alter your will to include funds to help pay for a new grandchild's education.

As you grow older and accumulate wealth, you should also review insurance policies. You may no longer need to pay for the same protections you required in your thirties or forties.

Aging

You'll need to check in with your estate plan more often as you age. When named heirs, beneficiaries, agents, or representatives have passed away or can no longer handle your estate's responsibilities, it's time to designate someone new.

Pay close attention to long-term care planning and insurance policies. You'll need to think about where you'll live and who'll help take care of you if you need assistance. You also have to determine where the money will come from to pay for any needs beyond what insurance policies might cover.

Your financial situation may change. Money once earmarked for others may now be needed to pay for your care—or care for a spouse or family member. This may also be the time for creating an estate planning trust if you haven't already.

Remember, a time may come when you're no longer legally competent to make changes due to circumstances affecting your mental abilities. So, review your documents regularly to avoid potential issues.

CAN YOU DO IT YOURSELF?

DIY May Not Be Cheaper in the End

The Internet has made "DIY" a trendy acronym. Focusing on saving money and learning new skills, "do-it-yourself" has people from all generations taking on tasks they usually would have hired out.

While it may be safe to tackle some DIY projects on your own, it's smart to pause and reconsider your skill set when it comes to keeping you and your family safe. Saving a few bucks by DIYing an estate plan can be a risky move costing more time and money in the end.

THE LURE OF ONLINE SERVICE PROVIDERS

Several online providers offer inexpensive do-it-yourself options for wills and other estate planning documents. You can create advance healthcare directives and some other forms on your own. But potential cost savings from using online service providers or templates may not outweigh the risk when it comes to more involved wills and trusts. DIY estate planning is not for everyone. The complexity of your assets and personal and family circumstances should drive your decision.

Seeking professional help from an estate planning attorney might be a smarter move in more complicated situations, such as a dependent with special needs, intricate real estate holdings, or owning a business. An experienced attorney won't just advise you on legal matters but can also counsel you through making any delicate decisions.

Should You DIY Estate Planning?

Surveys over the past decade report that most adults in the US do not have wills to direct distribution of their assets after death. While the majority of people have not prepared any estate planning paperwork, many understand the importance of doing so. People fail to seek help from attorneys because they're intimidated by the process, concerned about the cost, or both.

The broad availability of do-it-yourself wills online may tempt people because of their simplicity and low price.

To complete a DIY will, you simply need to fill in the blanks and enter your credit card details. But if you decide to create one this way, understand that the provider's services are not a substitute for legal advice. If you're not careful, any mistakes made could have lasting consequences for you and your family.

Online DIY Estate Planning Providers

Selecting an online DIY estate planning provider can seem overwhelming because of the rapidly growing number of services available on the Internet.

One of the most well-known DIY providers is LegalZoom.com. LegalZoom allows you to create a basic DIY will for a flat fee. For a small upcharge, you can add on two weeks of legal consulting from their network of attorneys. A bundle package is also available that includes a simple will, durable financial power of attorney, living will, and one year of legal consultations.

Other popular DIY estate planning service providers include RocketLawyer.com, Nolo.com, LawDepot.com, Gentreo.com, and TrustandWill.com. These companies provide various services, including premium plans, legal service subscription options, and a menu of pay-per-document pricing options.

Regardless of the DIY provider you consider, you'll find them promoting low rates for legal documents that cost substantially more when prepared by a lawyer. However, completing a DIY will is not the same as comprehensive estate planning.

A large part of planning requires careful consideration of important questions about your assets, family circumstances, and legal requirements in your state. You want a set of documents that will hold up to any challenges in court so your wishes are followed. If someone questions your choices and contests your will after your death, legal fees can become significant. These expenses can cut into the assets you leave behind or cost your loved ones out of pocket.

Your estate might also include more complex issues than you realize. If you do prepare a DIY will or other legal documents, consider hiring a local estate planning attorney to review them. They can help determine whether you need to make any changes or if you need to create any additional documents.

IS A DIY ESTATE PLAN A GOOD CHOICE FOR YOU?

There are certain situations in which going the DIY route might be appropriate. If you're single with modest possessions or have only one surviving relative to receive assets, DIY estate planning might make sense.

Using an online service to create a will introduces risks that could impact asset distribution and cause significant family tension in more complex situations.

Mistakenly leaving someone or something out of your will or making other mistakes in a DIY document could risk a legal challenge.

When a court determines a will invalid, it's as if it doesn't exist. You're then considered intestate: someone who died without a will. This means you don't have a say in who gets your stuff or who's the guardian of your kids. State intestacy laws and a judge control those decisions. You'll learn more about intestacy (and why you want to avoid it) in Chapter 4.

While a DIY estate plan may not be a perfect solution, it's better than dying without a will.

Do Your Homework Before You DIY

Keep in mind, online providers are businesses that need to make money. They support low-cost or free services by including extra charges for additional documents you likely need or an ongoing subscription you may forget to cancel. Also, be aware, positive online reviews may consist of links paying affiliate commissions.

OTHER ESTATE PLANNING DOCUMENTS

When you think about a comprehensive estate plan, other legal documents might be necessary. For example, there are documents to assign someone the ability to make financial or medical decisions if a severe injury or illness leaves you unable to communicate them yourself.

When you have a blended family or a family member with special needs, creating a specialized trust may be in order. While DIY software is available for some of these documents, establishing trusts to function as you intend is a complex process and better handled by an estate lawyer.

DIY estate planning services are not a one-size-fits-all solution. However, if you have a simple situation with few assets, it might be the right approach to take. The next section and following chapters can better equip you to decide.

WHY HIRE AN ATTORNEY?

Peace of Mind That Your Wishes Will Be Followed

Creating your estate plan on your own is not a good idea in many cases. Hiring an estate planning lawyer may be in your best interests when you have dependents, complex or substantial assets, a blended family, or a child with special needs.

WHERE AN ATTORNEY CAN HELP

Here are eight reasons to consider retaining an estate planning attorney instead of trying to DIY your plan.

#1: Assistance with Avoiding Probate

Without a good plan, your estate will go through the probate court system after you die. During this time, your assets will be identified, your debts will be paid off, and beneficiaries will receive distributions of assets. The probate process is public, can take months to several years, and can be expensive. However, with careful planning, you can significantly minimize the need for probate.

An attorney can either help you designate beneficiaries for specific assets or create a trust to avoid the probate process. The nuances associated with probate are complicated, but the attorney you hire in your state should be current in the process.

#2: Help with Protecting Your Assets, Yourself, and Your Family

Dealing with your incapacitation or passing will be difficult for family members. Your lawyer can include legal requisites in your plan to ensure assets pass to the people or organizations you desire. They can also help you nominate a guardian to care for minor children upon your death and set up documents allowing control of when and under what conditions heirs receive assets.

Using the wrong words, forgetting signatures, and failing to follow the state's requirements for witnesses are reasons a DIY estate plan could leave your family without protection. An attorney can help avoid simple mistakes that could have unintended and costly consequences.

Same-Sex and Unmarried Couples

When creating an estate plan, same-sex and unmarried couples face unique challenges due to evolving legislation regarding these unions. An experienced attorney understands current laws affecting these relationships and develops estate planning documents reflecting the couple's wishes while protecting each partner's interests in the estate.

#3: Saving Time While Avoiding Common Errors

When creating a plan, you'll be organizing your wishes and records. This makes it easier for your family to find essential documents, insurance policies, titles, and beneficiary designations after your passing. The planning process can also help find and fix mistakes while you're still able to correct them.

Working with an estate planning attorney can help you avoid the following common mistakes:

- Failing to designate beneficiaries
- Dying without a will or estate plan
- Creating an inadequate plan

- Accidental disinheritance
- Forgetting to include certain assets
- Failing to modify a plan as changes and life events occur

You'll save time working with a lawyer to create a comprehensive plan, and it may save money in the end. If problems force your family to use the court system to fix DIY estate documents, this process can quickly become expensive.

#4: Creating a Special Needs Trust

When you have a loved one with special needs, an attorney can ensure they'll be cared for by creating a special needs trust. This type of trust helps you provide for someone with a disability while protecting their ability to continue receiving public benefits, including Social Security Disability Insurance (SSDI), Supplemental Security Income (SSI), Medicare, and Medicaid. Without a special needs trust, your loved one could lose benefits when they inherit assets from your estate.

#5: Taking an Objective Look

Creating your estate documents can be emotional, and family dynamics can make it difficult to determine the right strategy. Do you split things up equally? Or is there a way to distribute your assets fairly even though that may mean unequal dollar values? An attorney specializing in estate planning will help you answer these questions and more by taking an objective look at your estate, goals, and family's future needs.

#6: Understanding Testacy and Guardianship Laws

Creating a plan with an experienced lawyer helps you be sure the right tools are used to make your final wishes known. With all the i's dotted and t's crossed, you'll be confident your minor children are cared for and your assets are going to your chosen beneficiaries.

#7: Reducing Your Tax Liabilities

The Tax Cuts and Jobs Act (TCJA) temporarily increased the federal exemption from estate taxes through 2025. If you pass away in the next few years, your estate might avoid federal estate and gift taxes unless its value is substantial. After 2025, the temporary increase is set to expire. The federal estate and gift tax exemption should return to its pre-TCJA levels.

Your estate may be liable for federal estate taxes depending on its gross value, liabilities, eligible deductions, and settlement expenses. If a net estate exceeds the federal estate tax exemption, family members are responsible for the federal estate tax.

An attorney can help you understand the state and federal estate tax laws to reduce the taxes your family might otherwise have to pay.

#8: Peace of Mind

An inclusive estate plan is one of the best things you can do for loved ones and yourself. By retaining an experienced lawyer, you can ensure your documents are prepared correctly so they're legally followed. Plus, as life happens and changes in circumstances require you to amend your plan, an attorney can make sure your needs and wishes continue to be covered through proper updating of your legal paperwork.

A proper estate plan could make the transition your family experiences after your death much smoother. It can also help them avoid substantial expenses and allow for the speedy administration of your estate. While it may cost more upfront, the resulting benefit of using an attorney can be well worth the expense.

Chapter 2

Determining Your Estate

Most of us don't consider estate planning until after we amass substantial assets, if at all. But in addition to safeguarding our medical care and finances in emergency cases, key aspects of estate planning are building, preserving, and transferring wealth. This becomes necessary once we accumulate money, investments, real estate, and possessions we want to protect and eventually sell, pass on to heirs, or donate. In other words, estate planning isn't just for the wealthy. It's for everyone.

YOUR FINANCIAL HOUSE

Maximizing Net Worth, Minimizing Taxes

Estate planning involves creating goals and strategies to provide financially for you and those you care about, plus the distribution of assets upon your passing. So it affects your financial planning throughout your life.

You can think of financial planning as the blueprints for building your estate, aka financial house. The parts of your financial plan are like the areas and systems of a home. Each one has a purpose. Yet without considering them as a whole, building them on a solid foundation, and protecting them from outside risks, your estate will be as fragile as a house of cards.

FINANCIAL PLANNING

In broad terms, the financial planning process defines your current economic situation. It creates goals, objectives, strategies, and tactics to address future financial needs. This may also include meeting the potential needs of any dependents, family, friends, business partners, or charities near and dear to you.

Financial planning consists of strategizing for investing, education, retirement, insurance, risk management, employee benefits, taxes, and estates. It involves determining the activities, assets, and timings most appropriate for achieving your goals under personal circumstances and widespread economic conditions.

Investing, Education, and Retirement Planning

Creating an investment strategy begins with assessing your current financial situation and setting goals for where you want to go. Education planning and retirement planning are major subsets aligned with investment planning.

Your core values, money beliefs, priorities, temperament for risk, and need for access to funds all come into play when creating your investment-plan goals. Once goals are determined, you can develop objectives and strategies to meet them.

There are many different asset classes to invest in to meet financial goals. Each asset class has its unique characteristics, including its risk-reward potential. A solid investment plan usually contains these most common types: cash, stocks (equities), bonds (fixed income), and real property.

Goals, time horizons, and the level of risk you can tolerate determine the assets in which you invest. This is known as asset allocation. The percentage of each asset you hold and the various investments you own within the asset class is known as diversification.

Risk Tolerance versus Risk Capacity

Risk tolerance is the amount of risk you're willing to take, based on logic and emotions. Risk capacity is the amount of risk you can take—or need to take—before it threatens your ability to meet financial goals. Together they determine how you should invest.

We invest for college, retirement, and other long-term goals. So it's essential to regularly monitor and evaluate our investments to ensure we stay on the right track to achieve them. It's also critical to change our plans in various life stages and after events such as marriage, births, divorce, career change, retirement, and advanced aging. Making necessary adjustments due to significant life happenings or changing economic conditions will help you continue progressing toward long-term objectives.

How and where you invest and whether the money you invest with is pre- or post-tax can make a difference in estate planning. You also need to understand the ownership rights, survivorship rights, and tax implications of all your investments. The more you know, the easier it will be to ensure assets remain with or are gifted to those you have chosen upon your death.

Insurance Planning and Risk Management

Life is risky. While we can't avoid all risks, we can manage them and even insure against some. Adequate insurance is often your best protection against financial losses. Some coverage is required. Others, such as protection for income and economic well-being, are optional. They can all help to manage risk and protect your income and assets.

Employee Benefits Planning

Employer-provided benefits can play a significant role in helping you build and protect your financial house. This planning involves evaluating the compensation and benefits options offered by your employer (and your spouse's, if applicable), such as:

- Group insurance plans: medical, dental, vision, life, and disability
- Access to supplemental coverages: i.e., life, accident, cancer
- Pensions and retirement savings plans
- Employee stock options and profit-sharing programs

- Flexible spending accounts (FSAs) and health savings accounts (HSAs)
- Tuition reimbursement, continuing education and training, licensure fees
- Employee assistance programs: legal, wellness, counseling

You'll want to coordinate the selection of your employee benefits (and a spouse's, if relevant) with other areas of your financial plan; namely investment, insurance, retirement, tax, and estate planning.

Tax Planning

Arranging your finances in a tax-efficient manner can help minimize the federal, state, or local taxes you pay. Knowing upfront the tax implications of any income you earn can reduce your annual tax bill and lessen future tax liabilities for years to come.

Short- and long-term tax planning strategies may involve:

- Determining the best filing status and taking advantage of eligible tax deductions and credits
- Using tax-advantaged savings and investing accounts such as:
  - 401(k)s, 403(b)s, and 457(b)s
  - Individual retirement accounts (IRAs)
  - 529s or other education savings accounts
  - Medical or dependent care flexible spending accounts (FSAs)
  - Health savings accounts (HSAs)
- Qualified charitable donations
- Tax gain-loss harvesting on investments
- Gifting assets
- Establishing trusts

WHAT IS AND ISN'T SUBJECT TO PROBATE

Keeping the Court's Hands Off Your Stuff

Upon death, your estate is settled through a process termed "probate." Whether you die with a will (testate) or without a will (intestate), the probate court oversees the settlement, unless your estate is minimal or you take additional steps to avoid probate. State laws do vary, so you must check your state's particulars when doing estate planning.

YOUR ASSETS AND PROBATE

Your estate contains all the things you leave behind. It may include a house or other real property, bank accounts, clothing, jewelry, antiques, personal items, a business, and investments.

While the legal process varies from state to state, what happens to assets when you die depends on what those belongings are and whether you create a will or trust before your passing. But some of your money and possessions can skip the probate process altogether.

Probate Origin

The earliest known usage of the English noun *probate* was in the 1400s to define "the official proving of a will." It comes from the Latin verb *probare*, which means "to try, test, prove, and examine." *Reprobate* means "not proven" or "disapprove," whereas *approbate* means "approve" or "accept as legal and genuine."

WHAT PASSES THROUGH PROBATE

Assets solely owned by a deceased person become part of an estate and must go through the probate process. The personal representative you name in your will oversees your estate and distributes assets according to your wishes. Without a will, the court assigns an estate representative to transfer ownership according to state intestacy laws.

Individually Owned Assets

Assets in your name only, or items without a title or document of ownership, are considered individually owned assets. Furniture, heirlooms, personal possessions, bank and investment accounts, vehicles, and real estate can all fall into this classification.

Tenants-in-Common Assets

When two or more people own property, they may own it as tenants in common. With this arrangement, each individual possesses a percentage interest in the property. The ownership split might be a fifty-fifty arrangement, a sixty-forty, or even a thirty-thirty-forty with multiple owners. Tenancy in common is frequently used when individuals purchase real estate with someone other than a spouse.

In tenants-in-common situations, the deceased's property ownership percentage transfers to their heirs and not the other owner(s) of the asset. The property goes through the probate court system to ensure a proper change of ownership.

Assets with No Beneficiary or a Predeceased Beneficiary

Certain assets, like life insurance policies or retirement accounts, allow you to name a beneficiary. This allows for an easy payout when you pass away because those assets are not probated.

If you fail to list that a beneficiary or a named heir is also deceased, the asset becomes part of your probate estate and must go through the court process.

Assets Not Held in a Trust

A living trust, which you'll learn more about in Chapter 5, is one way to keep control over your property and stay out of probate court. But it works only for the assets you remember to put into the trust. Assets you accumulate that do not get placed in the trust must be probated.

WHAT AVOIDS PROBATE

When possible, limiting probate makes sense. By taking proper actions ahead of time, you can reduce the burden on surviving heirs. Skipping probate also keeps your matters private and avoids costly fees and taxes.

There are several steps you can take before death to keep assets out of probate. Some are easy and can and should be done right away. Others may involve more time and effort and may not be necessary until your financial house is of considerable size.

Proper Beneficiary Designation

Correctly naming beneficiaries and contingent beneficiaries on insurance policies, trusts, financial accounts, investment accounts, and retirement accounts allows those assets to skip the probate process.

Life insurance policies you hold allow you to name one or more beneficiaries to receive policy proceeds upon your death. It's also wise to name alternate beneficiaries to avoid problems should your primary beneficiary die with or before you.

Payable on Death (POD) and Transfer on Death (TOD) Accounts

For accounts held at banks and credit unions, a payable on death (POD) arrangement, also known as a Totten trust, allows you to name beneficiaries on those accounts. It's free and easy to convert an account to a POD. Simply ask your financial institution for the form to complete.

A POD will not entitle a beneficiary or beneficiaries to any of the funds in the account when you—or a joint account holder—are alive. But upon the last account holder's death, the beneficiaries automatically become the account owners, skipping the probate process.

A transfer on death (TOD) is similar to a POD, but you use it with investment and retirement accounts, including 401(k)s, IRAs, brokerage accounts, and individual stocks and bonds. Some states may also allow a TOD arrangement on vehicles and real estate.

Depending on specific state laws, these accounts may transfer to your surviving spouse first and then on to TOD beneficiaries upon their death. You can revoke or change a beneficiary on POD and TOD arrangements at any time before you pass away as long as you've not been deemed mentally incompetent.

Because these designations help assets skip probate, they take precedence over language in a will. That's why it's essential to designate the individual or individuals you want to receive them as the beneficiary.

Revocable Living Trusts

A revocable living trust can be an effective instrument in your estate planning. With one in place, you can avoid probate, maintain privacy, retain control of assets until death or incapacitation, and efficiently transfer assets to heirs. A living trust is more difficult and costly to establish, but it provides the flexibility a will cannot. Chapter 5 is devoted entirely to addressing trusts and focuses on creating and using a living trust.

Jointly Owned Property

Other assets that skip probate include those held jointly. Joint ownership can get a little tricky and depends on your state of residency. Still, there are a few types: joint tenancy with rights of survivorship, tenancy by the entirety, tenancy in common, and community property. We'll discuss the particulars of each in the next section of this chapter.

ENSURING PROPER OWNERSHIP RIGHTS

Little Effort Required, but Details Are Important

Owning an asset jointly is one of the simplest ways to keep it out of probate. But joint ownership can also limit your rights and options if you want to transfer ownership.

You can hold title to personal and real property jointly in four different ways: tenancy in common, joint tenancy with rights of survivorship, tenancy by the entirety, and community property.

Joint ownership is easy to create, but it's critical to follow the law in your state. Because property rights vary, be sure you understand those of the state where the property is located if it is different than where you reside.

TENANCY IN COMMON

With a tenancy in common, two or more individuals own a percentage interest in a titled property. In some states, the percentage must be equal. But an unequal portion is allowed in most states. For instance, one tenant might own 40 percent of the property, another owns 35 percent, and a third owns the remaining 25 percent.

While each owner has less than 100 percent financial ownership of the asset, they each have the full right to occupy and use the entire property. They also share the total liability of any debts or taxes due on the property.

Real Property versus Personal Property

Real property includes land and permanent natural or human-made additions, such as trees, waterways, and buildings, as well as the rights of use, control, and disposition of the land and its attachments. Personal property is all moveable items you can touch and feel, or intangible items with value, like intellectual property.

Because tenants in common hold ownership individually, they can transfer their interest in the property however they desire. This can include selling a share or leaving it to heirs in a will. Through purchase or inheritance, the new owner becomes a tenant in common with the other owners.

A key takeaway here is that the other owners in tenants-in-common arrangements do not automatically inherit a deceased owner's share. Instead, its distribution is according to a will, trust, or intestacy law.

JOINT TENANCY WITH RIGHTS OF SURVIVORSHIP (JTWROS)

With joint tenancy, individual owners must have an equal ownership interest in the property (except in Colorado, Connecticut, Ohio, or Vermont). The title document for the property must state the intent of survivorship rights. A common way to say this is that the property is held "as joint tenants with rights of survivorship," abbreviated as JTWROS.

When two or more people are JTWROS, their interest in the property transfers to the remaining survivors upon their passing. This type of property transfer occurs automatically according to law, outside of probate court. Rights of survivorship are often used for ownership in real estate, vehicles, and financial accounts.

Like tenancy in common, a disadvantage to joint tenancy is the full liability for debts and taxes. If one tenant fails to pay a debt, creditors can sue to have the property sold, even if another owner objects.

TENANCY BY THE ENTIRETY

A form of tenancy generally only available to married couples, and only available in some states, is tenancy by the entirety. In this arrangement, each spouse is presumed to own and have full use of the entire property. Neither can sell or transfer their ownership in the property without consent from the other. At the time of one spouse's death, total ownership transfers to the remaining spouse.

Tenancy by the entirety applies only when acquiring assets after the owners are wed or when retitling property individually owned before the marriage to include the names of both spouses once married.

The following states currently allow for this type of ownership: Alaska, Arkansas, Delaware, Florida, Hawaii, Illinois, Indiana, Kentucky, Maryland, Massachusetts, Michigan, Mississippi, Missouri, New Jersey, New York, North Carolina, Ohio, Oklahoma, Oregon, Pennsylvania, Rhode Island, Tennessee, Vermont, Virginia, and Wyoming. While some only recognize this ownership on real estate, other states do so for all property, so check your state for specifics.

A primary advantage of tenancy by the entirety is that creditors of one spouse cannot force the property's sale to recover debts unless both spouses consent. Creditors may place a lien on property held in tenancy by the entirety. Still, if the debtor passes before the other spouse, the remaining spouse takes ownership of the property free and clear of the debt. Signatures from both spouses are required on a mortgage for tenancy by the entirety property, so both can be held liable for mortgage debt.

COMMUNITY PROPERTY

Community property is an additional type of joint ownership. It applies to married couples only in a handful of states. At the time of this writing, they are Arizona, California, Idaho, Louisiana, Nevada, New Mexico, Texas, Washington, and Wisconsin. The states of Alaska, Tennessee, and South Dakota have an elective community property law enabling spouses to opt in to the community property system or designate specific assets as community property. Since rules can change, verify the current property laws with your state.

Assets considered community property, also known as marital property, are everything a married couple owns together. This includes all income, assets, and liabilities during the marriage, no matter who earned, bought, sold, or signed on the bottom line.

Assets and debts acquired before marriage are not usually considered community property, nor are gifted or inherited assets given to one spouse. But property brought into a marital union can become community property when adding the new spouse to the title or deed.

Generally, under community property laws, each spouse receives an equal division of community property in the event of divorce. In some states, a judge may choose to divide assets between spouses in any percentage they deem equitable.

Some community property states allow for "community property with right of survivorship" to avoid probate. In this case, when one spouse dies their half of the property passes directly to the surviving spouse. Otherwise, each spouse in a community property state is entitled to choose who inherits their half of property assets through a will or trust. When a spouse dies intestate in a community property state, their 50 percent transfers to their surviving spouse.

DOCUMENTING AND GROWING YOUR NET WORTH

Inventory: What You Own and Owe and a Plan to Widen the Gap

To prepare a thorough estate plan, you need to identify your assets (everything you own) and your liabilities (everything you owe). What you owe needs to be paid, and what you own can be given to others as gifts or to provide for their care. In addition to determining your net worth (assets minus liabilities), you'll also want to make sure you have a solid understanding of your cash flow (income minus expenses).

Armed with that financial information, you can create goals to widen the gap between what you earn and spend—and what you own and owe. Or you can take other steps to meet your financial needs and the needs of those you care about.

DETERMINING FINANCIAL NET WORTH

While it might take some effort to create a detailed inventory of your finances, you'll thank yourself later. The sooner you open up a spreadsheet or document on your computer or grab a notebook and pencil, the better. It's up to you how much detail to include. Just remember, the more you list, the easier it will make things for you, your loved ones, and anyone you may hire to assist with your financial and estate planning.

What You Own

At a minimum, include a description of the property, how it's owned (individually or jointly), the market value of the asset, and the market value of your current ownership in the joint property as applicable.

Market Value

Fair market value (FMV) is the price a property would sell for on the open market. It's the price you'd agree to sell to a willing buyer when you both know all relevant facts, without either of you having to execute the transaction.

For example:

INVENTORY OF ASSETS: COMPILED MM/YYYY				
DESCRIPTION	OWNERSHIP TYPE	PERCENT OWNED	ASSET MARKET VALUE	OWNERSHIP MARKET VALUE
Savings Account at Main Street Bank, Account #15-234-7839	Individual	100 percent	$10,000	$10,000
Real estate located at: 123 E. Main St. Somewhere, NY 12345	Jointly Owned, Tenants in Common with: Sarah A. Smythe	50 percent	$200,000	$100,000
Roth IRA, Vanguard	Individual	100 percent	$12,500	$12,500
Total Ownership Value of Assets			$222,500	$122,500

Assets you may want to list in your inventory include:

- Liquid assets: cash, savings and checking accounts, money market accounts, certificates of deposit, easily tradable stocks and bonds, etc.
- Retirement accounts: 401(k)s, 403(b)s, IRAs, pensions, annuities, death benefits

- Alternative investments: precious metals, art and antiques, other collectibles of value
- Employee stock options or deferred compensation
- Real estate
- Vehicles
- Money owed to you via personal loans or private mortgages
- Life insurance policies with cash value
- Digital assets and frequent flyer miles or credit card reward points
- Other personal property: electronics, household items, jewelry, furs, tools, equipment, clothing, livestock
- Business assets
- Intellectual property

What You Owe

In this section, provide the details of any debts you have.

INVENTORY OF LIABILITIES: COMPILED MM/YYYY	
DESCRIPTION	**DEBT OWED**
Mortgage at ABC Bank, Loan #825-4329567, on the property at: 123 E. Main St. Somewhere, NY 12345	$50,000
Student Loan, #789123-edu	$23,000
Total	$73,000

Liabilities to list include:

- Mortgages
- Vehicle loans
- Student loans
- Personal loans

- Major credit cards
- Other liabilities: legal judgments, outstanding child support, other personal debts

Calculate Your Net Worth

Assets – Liabilities = Net Worth

From our previous example: $122,500 – $73,000 = $49,500

With staggering student loans and high consumer debt levels, it's not unheard of for people to have a negative net worth. But with the accumulation of assets and paying down debts, net worth increases. The pace at which that happens is largely dependent on cash flow, or the rate at which income comes in compared to expenses going out.

What you do with your net cash flow, also known as discretionary income, can be pivotal to your financial health and long-term financial plans. Spending some on vacations, entertainment, and fun activities is okay. Yet spending all your extra income on non–wealth-building activities won't help you reach financial goals.

WIDENING THE GAPS

To increase net cash flow, you must widen the gap between your income and expenses. Then, using the higher cash flow to both invest and pay down debts, you expand the gap between your assets and liabilities. This increases your net worth. Why is that important? So you can take care of the future you and those you provide for.

What Comes In and What Goes Out

You must know what your income and expenses are before you can widen the gap between them. Tracking all the money coming in and going out of your household for three months should provide what you need to know. But don't forget any expenses or income you pay or receive annually or semiannually. Several financial apps can help with this, including Mint, PocketGuard, Albert, Zeta, and Tiller. You can also keep track in a spreadsheet or notebook.

Putting Your Money to Work

Once you have a good picture of how money flows in and out, you can prepare a budget. While the word "budget" gets a bad rap, it's an important planning tool to help direct money where you want it to go. If you don't like the word "budget," try naming it a "spending plan" or a "wealth-building plan."

The purpose of budgeting is to focus on making intentional saving and spending decisions based on financial goals. Some people use a very detailed budget and record all their financial transactions. We're not asking you to do that, unless it will help you stay focused. But we suggest keeping tabs on your spending plan to ensure money is going where you want to achieve your short- and long-term goals.

Work the Gap

Reducing expenses and unnecessary spending is a quick way to widen the gap and increase your net cash flow. Those additional funds can then help pay off loans faster and boost your contributions to savings and investment accounts. But you'll also want to give adequate attention to increasing your income. Earning more and spending less is a powerful combination to speed up progress toward financial targets.

INSURING YOUR INCOME AND ASSETS

Security Against What If's

Because life is unpredictable, we often hear advice to prepare for a rainy day or build an emergency fund. While this is excellent guidance, it would be tough—if not impossible—to save enough for every potential accident, crisis, or "what if" situation we might face.

Enter insurance.

Insurance Has a Long History

Historical documents indicate the first known form of insurance was used in 1000 B.C.E., and was known as the Rhodian Sea Law. It evolved through the centuries, eventually making its way to the United States. The first insurance institutions in America were established in the early 1730s.

DETERMINE YOUR RISK TOLERANCE LEVEL

People purchase insurance products as a form of risk management. When you choose not to insure something, you're assuming risk. Weighing the decision on buying optional insurance coverage should start with reviewing the amount of risk you and your family are willing to take.

As you review the various insurance options that follow, remember there's a price to pay for the peace of mind insurance coverage provides.

Yet not paying for it could be financially devastating if a severe illness, accident, early death, or other unfortunate event happens.

PROTECTING YOUR INCOME

Laws and lenders often mandate insurance coverage for motor vehicles and real property, as those coverages help protect others too. But paying premiums to insure income is something you decide.

You might be fortunate enough to work for an employer who provides some level of disability and life insurance coverage for you. Just be sure to evaluate if it's an adequate amount to meet your needs. Review any coverages you have as a benefit and consider the amount of risk you're comfortable assuming.

Insuring Against a Disability

When you're young, it's hard to fathom that an illness or injury could prevent you from working. But the Social Security Administration reports that more than 25 percent of twenty-year-olds today will be disabled before they become sixty-seven. Accidents and illnesses don't discriminate; they can happen to anybody.

Disability insurance can provide both short- and long-term income protection. It helps pay for day-to-day expenses if you become disabled and unable to perform work responsibilities.

Short-Term Disability Protection

Short-term disability insurance (STDI) covers you when a disability results from something such as an illness, injury, childbirth, or medically necessary procedure. Depending on policy specifics,

STDI may cover up to 80 percent of your gross income during the coverage period, generally 60–180 days.

Long-Term Disability Coverage

Long-term disability insurance (LTDI) pays a portion of your income, generally 60–70 percent, when you cannot work for an extended period due to a covered disability. LTDI typically kicks in when you've been restricted from performing work for more than 90–180 days. Because of this waiting period, you may elect to buy both STDI and LTDI. Depending on the coverage, LTDI may pay until you're able to return to work, are eligible for retirement, or reach age sixty-five.

Insuring Against Loss of Life

As with disability insurance, you may think life insurance is unnecessary because you're young or without dependents. But no matter your age or status, you should think about securing life insurance if someone else depends on your income or could suffer financially by your passing.

To determine how much coverage to purchase, consider the needs of those you support and how long you'll want to help them after you're gone. Other factors to review are your current debt load, accumulated savings, and investments. Also, think about any large future expenses you want to assist with, such as a child's wedding or a spouse's retirement.

Standard guidelines for figuring out life insurance needs include multiplying your gross salary by any (or all) of these methods:

- The number of years you want to provide support
- The number of years until your retirement
- The number 10

Then, compare numbers with results from various online life insurance calculators. You could also speak with a reputable financial professional or insurance agent to evaluate the dollar amount of coverage you should buy.

Types of Life Insurance

In addition to calculating how much insurance you want, you also need to decide on the type of coverage: term or permanent.

Term life insurance provides coverage over a five- to forty-year period. If you die while the policy is in effect, your beneficiary receives the payout. The policy expires if you do not pass away during the term. It may also be renewable according to policy particulars. Term insurance is excellent for filling a temporary life need, such as the years you're paying on a mortgage or when children are living at home. It's generally the only type of life insurance you'll need.

Alternatively, permanent insurance is designed to provide coverage for a lifetime. The most common type of permanent coverage is a whole life insurance policy. As long as you continue making payments, the policy remains in effect, and your beneficiaries will receive the payout upon your death. The additional benefit of a whole life policy is its ability to accumulate cash value over time. You can borrow against the cash value or even give up the policy and receive its cash-surrender value. But it can take decades to build up enough to borrow from it, and accessing this benefit comes with purchasing a more expensive and complicated policy than term insurance. If you'd like to consider a permanent policy, you can investigate it further and speak with a qualified financial professional to ensure you fully understand the pros and cons of these policies.

PROTECTING ASSETS

When you have a car, home, or apartment lease in your name, you likely have insurance coverage for those items. Now's a good time to review those policies to ensure the coverage is adequate for your needs and risk tolerance level. Remember, you want to find a balance between being underinsured with the potential for financial devastation and being overinsured and wasting money. One other thing to be mindful of as your assets grow is the potential need for increased liability insurance.

Rainy Day Coverage

Additional liability insurance coverage, known as umbrella insurance, goes above and beyond standard insurance policy limits. If you file an insurance claim and your financial liability exceeds your current coverage amount, an umbrella policy kicks in and covers the difference. Without an umbrella policy in place, you'll face having to pay the difference with your assets.

Umbrella policies can also provide coverage for liabilities other insurance policies don't. This can include lawsuits brought against you for libel or mental anguish. This coverage is also beneficial when you own things that could potentially injure others. Dogs, pools, trampolines, recreational vehicles, motorcycles, or other items can put your assets at risk if someone becomes injured.

What might surprise you is how little this additional coverage can cost. The Insurance Information Institute states a $1 million personal umbrella liability policy costs $150–$300 per year, with each additional million costing $50–$75 more, when adequate home and auto insurance is in place.

Even if you have little income or few assets to protect, consider purchasing the insurances mentioned earlier. You might not think the worst can happen, but you'll be grateful you're prepared if it does.

PLANNING FOR YOUR RETIREMENT

Designing the Future You Desire

Retirement planning is complex and not something we can cover in just a few pages in a book. This section will provide information on determining your retirement needs, types of savings and investment accounts to maximize income and reduce taxes, and the transfer of retirement assets upon death.

HOW MUCH WILL YOU NEED?

When you're decades away from retirement, it's not easy to know what you'll need when you get there. Yet, you need to predict future costs as best you can to aim for a goal. Start by reviewing your current annual spending and consider how expenses might change in retirement. Some may decrease or disappear; others may just start to show up or increase. Don't forget to factor in any additional one-time costs, such as purchasing an RV for traveling or an anniversary dream vacation. With an estimate of annual and one-time expenses in retirement, you can then determine a savings goal.

An often-mentioned guideline for calculating your retirement number is the 25x rule, where x equals your annual expenses. If you estimate spending $40,000 per year in retirement, you will need $1 million in invested funds available so you don't exhaust your savings before the end of thirty years. Some argue this rule is not conservative enough and recommend using 30–35x times your yearly expenses. Take into account your future one-time costs, longevity estimates, and ability to lower discretionary spending if necessary when crafting your exact strategy. After estimating how much money you'll need for retirement, the next step is figuring out where it's coming from.

The Trinity Study, aka the 4 Percent Rule or 25x Expenses Rule

The Trinity study is based on a paper written by three finance professors at Trinity University in 1998. It concludes that if a person can cover a year's expenses with 4 percent of their savings and investment assets, their portfolio could sufficiently cover a thirty-year retirement period.

SOURCES OF RETIREMENT INCOME

Chances are your grandparents support their retirement with company pensions and Social Security (SS). But saving for retirement began falling to individuals starting with the late baby boomers and Generation X.

Social Security

Many fear Social Security will be gone by the time they reach the traditional retirement age. Although it may look entirely different than it does today, it's unlikely it will dissolve completely. Depending on your current age and work history, you'll probably receive some Social Security income in the future. But the role it plays in your retirement income may be minor. For estimates of future benefits, visit www.ssa.gov.

Defined Benefit Pensions

Defined benefit retirement plans provide a pre-established fixed benefit to employees at retirement. Typically, employers make most contributions to these pension plans, but sometimes employee contributions are required or permitted. Defined benefit plans are often more complex and costly than employee-funded defined contribution plans.

Personal Retirement Savings

To incentivize you to save for retirement, the government allows you some tax advantages. Traditional (pre-tax accounts) defer tax payments on money you contribute into the future. This puts off any taxes due until you withdraw cash years down the road. You fund after-tax (Roth) accounts with money you've already paid taxes on. But you don't pay any tax on your investment gains when they're later withdrawn.

Individual, employer-sponsored, and self-employed retirement savings plans each have their own rules, such as contribution limits, the timing of withdrawals, and eligibility. We'll cover some basics next, but you can learn more at www.irs.gov/retirement-plans.

Individual Retirement Arrangements (IRAs)

An individual retirement arrangement, also known as an individual retirement account, or IRA, allows you to save for the future in both tax-advantaged ways. You may split IRA contributions between a traditional and a Roth. Still, combined contributions between these accounts cannot exceed annual limits.

TRADITIONAL IRA

A traditional IRA could be a good option when you're in a high tax bracket but expect to be in a lower one when you withdraw funds. Contributions to a traditional IRA are generally tax deductible. Still, those may be limited when you have access to an employer-sponsored retirement plan and your modified adjusted gross income (MAGI) exceeds a specific amount.

ROTH IRA

With a Roth IRA, you're contributing already taxed money. The Roth's advantage is that when you take qualified distributions from it, they'll be tax-free. You may contribute annually to a Roth IRA when you (or your spouse) have taxable earnings, and your MAGI is below certain income limits.

Employer-Sponsored Savings Plan 401(k), 403(b), 457(b)

The most common types of employer-sponsored savings plans are the traditional 401(k), 403(b), and 457(b). These defined contribution plans are mostly funded by you, the employee, while some employers make matching or additional contributions. Some employers also offer a Roth deferral option in these plans. The rules for these Roths are slightly different, so be sure to review your employer's plan documents and IRS rules.

TRADITIONAL 401(K)

A qualified 401(k) plan allows you to contribute a portion of your wages directly to a retirement account. These plans are usually offered to the employees of larger for-profit businesses. While investment options may vary by employer, you choose the amount of wages you contribute up to annual IRS limits and select how to invest those funds. Some employers may also contribute to your 401(k) account as part of your employee benefits.

403(B) PLANS

A 403(b) is similar to a 401(k). However, it's for employees of nonprofit, tax-exempt businesses such as churches and other religious organizations, hospitals, schools, or universities. Tax-deferred contributions are made to these accounts following the same rules and contribution limits as the 401(k).

457 PLANS

Like 403(b) plans, 457 plans are almost identical to 401(k) plans, except they're meant for employees of local and state governments or specific tax-exempt organizations. When your employer offers both the 403(b) or 401(k) and a 457 plan, you may fund both up to maximum limits. This allows you to double tax-advantaged contributions.

Plans for the Self-Employed

When you're self-employed, you have many similar retirement saving options as employees participating in bigger company plans. Choices include a Simplified Employee Pension (SEP), a Savings Incentive Match Plan for Employees (SIMPLE IRA), and the one-participant, or "solo," 401(k). Learn more about these options at www.irs.gov/retirement-plans/retirement-plans-for-self-employed-people.

RETIREMENT ACCOUNT BENEFICIARIES

You must designate beneficiaries on your retirement accounts and keep them updated. If you don't, assets in those accounts could become a part of your probate estate and may end up with someone other than who you'd like to have them. In most cases, you must name your spouse as a beneficiary unless they sign a waiver permitting you to designate another individual.

When beneficiaries inherit retirement accounts, they may have various options for how they'll assume ownership and when they must take distributions. Options and rules vary depending on if it's your spouse or someone else inheriting the account. But all beneficiaries of traditional retirement accounts must include taxable distributions they receive in their gross income and pay taxes due on the funds in the year received. Other rules exist for those inheriting Roth accounts. Find additional information on beneficiary requirements at www.irs.gov/retirement-plans/plan-participant-employee/retirement-topics-beneficiary.

LEAVING A LEGACY BEHIND

Positively Impacting Others

Leaving behind a legacy may not be something you're thinking about at this point. But considering it now can allow you to make a difference in others' lives in the future. An impactful legacy begins with you—who you are, how you live life, and how you make a difference in the world around you. Your financial wealth adds to that.

LEGACY PLANNING

Creating a legacy is your chance to give more than just money to those you care about. It's an opportunity to incorporate your guiding principles and beliefs with other estate planning goals. Legacy planning expands beyond essential estate planning because it widens the spotlight on what you leave to others. By sharing your morals and values along with financial gifts to loved ones or charitable organizations, you can extend goodwill in ways that make more than an economic impact.

A Financial Legacy

Whether you want to leave a large inheritance behind or exhaust most of your financial resources before death, putting together a plan can help you reach those goals. No matter what age you are, it's crucial to understand where your money is coming from, how you'll use it while alive, and what happens to it once you're gone.

Take care of yourself first, along with your spouse or committed partner and minor children. Then you can give gifts to others as you see fit, including adult children, other relatives, friends, and the community. But leaving a lasting legacy behind rarely happens, if ever, without a plan.

With that said, even with a strategy, you'll make mistakes. Every step you take may not always be forward, and that's okay. Those slipups and misdirections can teach you valuable lessons that you, in turn, can share with others. And sharing your experience and life learnings with your loved ones can be part of your legacy.

No rule says you must leave financial gifts behind. Yet if that's your desire, shouldn't you also leave behind the knowledge to manage them?

It can take decades to build wealth. But it can be lost in a matter of days by those who don't understand personal finance and money management. So, while living your life and raising a family, along with accumulating savings and investments, teach those behind you. Teaching money lessons to children can start at a very young age (and your elders are never too old to learn!).

Talking to Your Parents about Their Estate

Speaking with your parents about their finances and estate plans can be challenging. If they're reluctant, start with short conversations focusing on making sure they're protected and their final wishes are known. But don't put this task off; it only gets more difficult as time goes on.

Charitable Impact

Do you want to make a difference beyond your family lines? Charitable donations to organizations you care about can impact the lives of many. While you may give to these organizations throughout your lifetime, you might also want to include them in your final giving. Details for how you can go about doing that through tools such as donor-advised funds are included in later chapters.

Gifts That Keep on Giving

The legacy gifts you leave to others can be more than just money, property, or other financial resources. Passing along your ethics, ideals, good habits, talents, and family traditions are gifts that can keep on giving.

Money is a tool that helps you achieve financial and life goals. Your values and morals guide your actions, and good habits help you stay disciplined to reach those goals. You can pass on these principles to family and friends through letters, stories, your interactions with them, and your relationships with others.

Because you won't always be here, take time now to share and teach your unique talents. Practice old family traditions and put an unusual twist on some to make new ones. Explain your family's roots and document your family tree. Watch old family videos and flip through picture albums. Don't let cherished and meaningful memories die along with you.

The greatest gifts you can give someone are time together, loving relationships, and experiences that create lasting memories. While money in the bank can help provide for them, who you are and what you do can impact them forever.

YOU CAN START NOW

While you might only be able to gift your time and talents today, there's no need to delay doing so. You can start positively impacting others now. As you build your estate, you may be able to make more significant financial impacts. But again, the best things you can give to the people and organizations you care about are not always measured in dollars.

When you're looking to build generational wealth or make a sizable charitable donation, it may take time and effort. But you can make progress on that goal by getting started today. Remember, leaving a legacy doesn't often happen by chance. See Chapter 8 for more on legacy planning.

Chapter 3

Taking Care of You

There's a good chance you'll spend some (or most!) of your adult life taking care of or helping others. If you have children, care for an aging relative, work in a helping profession, or volunteer for nonprofits, the needs of others may often be your focus. While much of estate planning deals with how to support others when you're gone, it's also about putting yourself first and making sure you're meeting your needs and desires. It's like the "oxygen mask" analogy. You can better support the people who matter to you after taking care of yourself first.

To do this, you'll want to think long term. You need to make plans for your health and finances. What would your wants and needs be should something happen that leaves you unable to communicate or make critical decisions independently? This chapter covers these sensitive but serious topics to address when developing your estate plan.

SAFEGUARDING YOUR ESTATE

Protecting Your Financial House

You spend a lifetime working to grow your estate to take care of yourself and even provide for others when you're gone. While your plan to build wealth over the years may be working, failing to make sure your financial house is secure is a risky move. If you aren't careful, plenty of things can happen that'll separate you from some (or even all) of your money.

To be sure you have the right protections in place to keep your estate secure, you need to identify situations that could negatively impact your net worth. Then you can be proactive about using financial and legal tools to safeguard assets. If you fail to act and something unforeseen happens to you, it may be too late for security measures.

THREATS TO YOUR FINANCIAL HOUSE AND HOW TO PROTECT IT

Protecting yourself against a job loss, divorce, severe illness or injury, or lawsuit should be your focus as you acquire assets. You can't control every situation you'll face. Still, you need to understand potential threats and take actions to safeguard your estate against possible problems.

Job Loss

No matter how secure your career feels or how much you enjoy it, there's likely some chance of a job loss. A change in management, corporate restructuring, or a poor annual review could cost you a paycheck and employee benefits.

You can take steps to protect your finances as you're building a nest egg during your working years. First, be a model employee who's open to change. Take annual evaluations seriously and work to remedy issues or improve upon anything highlighted as an area for growth. Stay current in your field and seek advanced training, certificates, or degrees. Take advantage of networking opportunities outside of the company picnic or holiday party, and consider diversifying income options by starting a small business.

Maintain an emergency fund that covers a minimum of three to six months of your expenses. Think about saving more if you're the sole breadwinner and your job is the only income source. Always invest enough in your 401(k) or similar plan to get any match your company offers. Aim to invest at least 15 percent of your pre-tax income. Start investing as early as possible to allow compound interest to work its magic. If you plan to work into your late sixties or seventies, you might think again. If you want to work at that age, that's great. But many people plan to do that and can't because of illness, disability, or corporate downsizing. When you still want to prepare for working in your senior years, investigate whether a low-cost annuity could create a secure retirement paycheck in the event of a job loss or other situation, leaving you unable to earn an income later in your career.

Divorce

One of the last things you want to think about when you're in love is your relationship ending. But realistically, many marriages end in divorce. If you've been through one or know someone who's divorced, you understand how financially devastating it can be. Everything you dreamed of having in retirement or leaving as a legacy to loved ones gets divided up. And lawyers make sure they get a cut too.

What can you do to help protect your heart and bank account? Start talking about money with your significant other before marriage. Both partners should participate in building a financial house as a couple. It should be a serious red flag if your partner tries to avoid the topic or wants to be solely in charge. Spend time boosting your financial literacy by reading personal finance books, listening to financial podcasts, or reading articles about managing money.

Consider a prenuptial agreement if either of you is bringing substantial assets or debts into the marriage. A postnuptial agreement might be a smart move if you're already married and experience a considerable change in your finances or relationship.

Serious Illness or Injury

We all hope to live a long and healthy life. Yet chances are you know someone with a devastating diagnosis or a life-changing injury they didn't anticipate or plan for financially.

Personal wellness is as essential as financial wellness. Focus on nutrition, exercise, and preventive healthcare. Maintain health insurance coverage and start a health savings account (HSA) if you're on a high-deductible medical insurance plan.

Skip risky DIY projects and hire professionals. Use safe driving practices to help avoid costly traffic tickets and accidents. Research disability and long-term care insurance and determine how they could help maintain your estate if you're seriously ill or injured. When appropriate, purchase term life insurance to help provide financial security and protect your estate for heirs if you die young.

Accidental Fatality

According to data from the CDC, unintentional injury is a leading cause of death in the United States. Three primary causes of death due to these accidental injuries include motor vehicle traffic, drug overdose, and falls.

Lawsuits

It's an unsettling thought, but you can get sued by anyone—with or without cause—throughout your adult life. Even if baseless claims are made against you, it can cost thousands of dollars in attorney and court fees to fight. As you might expect, the more assets you have, the greater the risk of being named in a lawsuit.

To avoid ending up in court, minimize risky behaviors that could harm others. Take care of your property so visitors don't suffer injuries. Always communicate professionally and avoid making negative social media posts. Know local laws and ordinances. Review increasing liability limits on your homeowners policy, check coverage limits on your car insurance, and consider an umbrella insurance policy. As you fill your financial house with assets, setting up a trust or gifting some assets might also make sense.

If you own a business, steer clear of unethical and illegal practices to reduce your risk of a lawsuit. Save your energy to address customers' concerns about products or services so you won't face legal complaints from them.

Know the laws related to your business and its operation. Work with an attorney so contracts are legal and carry adequate business insurance. Be sure to use the appropriate business structure as well. A limited liability company (LLC) or corporation separates your business from personal finances.

POWERS OF ATTORNEY

Giving Power While Protecting Yours

The security you feel when you have the right tools guarding your financial house is powerful. Still, preserving wealth and maintaining your estate may also require you to share that power with someone you trust. The estate planning tool that allows someone to legally act on your behalf is called a power of attorney (POA). There are POAs for different situations, so it's essential to understand the benefits and limitations of each before appointing anyone to this critical role.

CHOOSING THE POWER

POAs can be divided into two primary categories: financial and healthcare. A financial POA is a legal document through which you (the principal) grant the authority to act to an agent (also known as an attorney-in-fact). Your agent can be any person you trust and legally name. A healthcare POA is a legal document allowing your agent the authority to make decisions about your healthcare.

Beyond these, there are several types of POAs serving different purposes. Six kinds of POAs follow, with examples showing how important they are in protecting you, your estate, and those you love.

Durable Powers of Attorney

When you sign a durable POA, your agent can begin acting on the types of decisions you've granted them the authority to make. They also have the authority to continue acting on your behalf after you're incapacitated and are no longer able to make decisions yourself.

For example, you may suffer from advancing Alzheimer's disease or a traumatic brain injury from an automobile accident. When you cannot make your own decisions, your agent decides on the matters you granted them power over.

A DPOA can be used to handle all your affairs because it's not restricted to a specific transaction or period. However, you can revoke a DPOA by completing a revocation document, as long as you're legally competent. DPOAs automatically end when you pass away.

Naming Alternate POAs

Consider naming a second trusted person as an alternate to your designated agent on POAs. The alternate (successor) agent takes over if your agent cannot or refuses to act on your behalf. Avoid naming joint agents because of the potential for confusion and conflicts regarding decision-making.

Non-Durable Powers of Attorney

Non-durable POAs allow you to grant your agent the authority to make choices, sign documents, and manage day-to-day transactions. However, these POAs end, and your agent loses the power to act in your place if you're deemed incompetent. Instead, the court will appoint a conservator or guardian to make decisions on your behalf. (See Chapter 7 for rules on guardianships and conservatorships.)

General Powers of Attorney

General POAs are used to give agents broad authority to act. Under general POAs, your agent can make legal, real estate, financial, and business decisions you would otherwise make—although, some states may restrict the authority you can grant through general POAs.

Your general POA might buy and sell property, handle financial transactions, enter into and sign contracts, and pay bills for you. Since substantial control is given to an agent in a general POA, they're generally only appropriate for a short time when you can't manage your affairs.

For example, suppose you'll be traveling abroad for an extended time. In that case, a general POA might be an option, so someone oversees matters during your absence. Unless they're also durable, general POAs expire when you become incapacitated or die.

Limited Powers of Attorney

Limited POAs are also called special powers of attorney. These are legal documents through which you grant an agent the authority to act for you for a specific reason. For example, you might grant a limited POA to your sibling to allow him or her to sign checks for you to pay bills while you take three months to travel the world. However, your sibling will not be able to fully manage your finances or change all your investments to bitcoin.

Limited POAs can also be used for one-time transactions or to sell a piece of property. In this case, you might be ill and unable to finish the transaction but want to appoint someone to complete it for you. An agent with a limited POA cannot do anything else on your behalf other than complete the limited purpose outlined in the POA.

A limited POA ends when the transaction is complete or when the fixed time stated in the document concludes. For these reasons, some people create several limited POAs to give various agents authority to make different, specific decisions.

Springing Powers of Attorney

Springing POAs are not effective upon signing. Instead, they're implemented only when a triggering event occurs. For example, you might draft a springing POA to grant an agent the ability to act on your behalf when you're deployed on active duty. Many people prepare springing POAs that become effective only if they suffer an incapacitating illness or injury and are deemed incompetent by two doctors. A springing POA can be non-durable (ending at your incapacitation) or durable (ending at your death). You can use it to grant the agent authority to act in whatever ways you choose.

Medical or Healthcare Powers of Attorney

As part of an advance directive, a medical or healthcare POA gives you the ability to name an agent to make medical decisions on your behalf and assume control over your healthcare in cases of incapacitation.

Your healthcare agent will be able to consent to surgery, medical treatment, and releases of your medical records. He or she will also be able to decide whether you'll be given nutrition through a feeding tube and choose the healthcare facility where you'll receive treatment. Your medical POA is immediately effective upon signing. However, it can be used by your agent only if a doctor deems you to be incompetent.

WHEN DO YOU NEED A POA?

Adults over the age of eighteen should have POAs in place. When you draft a POA, you have control over who can make choices for you. If you become incapacitated, your family can avoid the lengthy and costly process of having a guardian or conservator appointed to act on your behalf. Other reasons to have POAs in place include extended travel or military deployment overseas and dangerous jobs. POAs can help protect your estate and keep financial and legal matters in order when you're unable to act.

ADVANCE HEALTHCARE DIRECTIVES

Sharing Your Wishes When You Cannot Speak for Yourself

When it comes to taking care of yourself, one of the most important things you can do is make decisions about medical care. This means determining the types of medical treatment you want to receive and naming someone to make critical healthcare decisions when you can't. The estate planning documents that address this are called advance healthcare directives. (We'll refer to them as advance directives for simplicity.) While they vary in form, name, and number from state to state, medical directives share your desires about end-of-life treatment.

People of every age suffer from severe illnesses and experience tragic accidents. Yet research suggests almost two-thirds of adults don't have these crucial documents. Unsurprisingly, older adults and those with chronic diseases are more likely to have healthcare directives. But assuming you want your wishes followed during a medical emergency, it's essential to learn more about these directives and take action to execute your state-specific forms.

DIFFERENT STATES, DIFFERENT REQUIREMENTS

Before getting into the specific details of medical directives, there are important terms you should know. Keep in mind there are numerous variations of titles used on documents in different states.

Important Terms to Know

- **Advance Directive:** This is the general term for documents explaining your healthcare preferences and designating someone to make medical decisions for you if you cannot do so.
- **Durable Power of Attorney for Healthcare:** This is a type of advance directive used when you can no longer communicate or choose for yourself. The person you appoint (your agent) will make medical decisions on your behalf using instructions in your directives. Your agent, or the individual you grant power of attorney, may also be called your healthcare representative, surrogate, or proxy.
- **Living Will:** This is another type of advance directive that informs physicians and loved ones about your preferences for medical treatment and care when you're unable to speak. Living wills typically include instructions regarding life-sustaining measures, organ donation, and pain management, along with other healthcare wishes.

State Specifics

Some states recognize just one document, an advance directive, which is essentially a durable power of attorney for healthcare and a living will combined.

Residents of other states must complete two separate healthcare directive documents: the living will for outlining healthcare wishes if you become incapacitated, and a DPOA for healthcare to designate someone to make medical treatment decisions for you.

Find requirements for your state by searching "advance directive" + "(your state)" and view government (.gov) sources.

NAMING A HEALTHCARE AGENT

The first step in creating an advance directive is choosing someone you trust to make healthcare judgments if you become incapacitated. You direct your agent to follow healthcare decisions in a living will or advance directive. Their role is consenting to or withholding medical procedures on your behalf. When your specific wishes are unknown, your agent may use their judgment to determine what aligns with your beliefs and is in your best interests.

While you may grant an agent the ability to make healthcare decisions, you can also place limits on their authority. For example, you could prevent them from consenting to an autopsy of your remains.

You have the option to designate just one healthcare agent, but consider naming an alternate agent as well. When your primary agent is unwilling or unable to make medical decisions for you, the alternate can legally take over.

MAKING DIFFICULT HEALTHCARE CHOICES

Creating healthcare directives requires tough choices about your medical care, including life support and organ donation. Additionally, you have the option to leave more instructions for doctors and family members about the treatment you're willing to receive.

Life Support

In a living will or advance directive, you can choose to be kept on life support to prolong life to the greatest extent possible.

Life-sustaining measures include mechanical ventilation, cardiopulmonary resuscitation (CPR), and artificial nutrition and hydration.

If you decide not to be kept on life support, you may choose specific situations where you would want it withheld, or to have life-sustaining measures stopped.

Examples of these qualifying conditions include:

- An incurable or irreversible condition in which death is imminent without life-sustaining treatment
- A permanent coma
- A persistent vegetative state

You may decide to forgo artificial life support in any of the previous circumstances. But you do have the option to select one or more conditions when you want life artificially prolonged.

Keep in mind, two physicians usually must agree with any diagnosis that impacts the use of a directive instructing life support to be withheld or withdrawn.

The Rules Change with Pregnancy

If you're pregnant when becoming incapacitated, medical staff may not follow your living will or advance directive. Most state laws require life-prolonging medical procedures to continue unless there's no chance the fetus will survive even with life support measures in place.

More Decisions after Refusing Life Support

If you decide against life-sustaining measures, you need to state whether you agree to artificial nutrition and hydration. Some people are against life support systems such as ventilators but opt to have tube feedings until death.

You also choose whether or not to receive pain medications when life support measures are refused or withdrawn. Comfort is an easy selection for most people, even if it delays death.

Organ Donation

Your preference to make anatomical gifts at the time of death is also part of your directive. It's necessary to determine which organs you're willing to donate and for what purposes.

You may donate specific body parts but have the option to give anything needed and medically acceptable. When you agree to donate, you'll need to state the purpose of your gift. Legally authorized purposes include transplantation, therapy, research, and education.

General Provisions and Witnesses

General provisions is the final section of an advance directive. It's there to ensure the document is legally recognized and valid. While these advance directives may be recognized in your state, be aware they may not legally bind a medical provider to follow them.

If you're eighteen years or older and understand the document's purpose and effect, you may legally execute a healthcare directive. Two legal adults must witness and declare you're of sound mind and not under duress or influence. The witnesses cannot be relatives, financially responsible for your medical care, or entitled to any part of your estate.

MORE ON ADVANCE DIRECTIVES

Answers to Frequently Asked Questions (FAQs)

Reading about healthcare directives may leave you with mixed emotions. Yet avoiding complicated feelings is one of the main reasons people don't have these documents in place. It's hard to think about being seriously ill and letting others take charge of your care. Planning for your final days may leave you questioning life choices and their impact on those you'll leave behind.

You may be nervous that you haven't determined who should make decisions for you or that you haven't shored up your financial house to support loved ones when you're gone. Or you might be anxious about end-of-life care wishes and sad thinking about death. Those feelings are valid. The estate planning process is distressing for some. But it's also essential, as it gives you control.

What follows are some frequently asked questions people have about preparing advance directives, along with answers to assist your planning.

BEFORE COMPLETING YOUR MEDICAL DIRECTIVES

As you begin researching medical directives and considering who to include in your plans, you're likely to have many questions about the logistics of completing the forms. Here are some of the most common questions people ask as they get started with the process.

Do I Need a Healthcare Directive Now?

Anyone over the age of eighteen should have advance directives. A severe illness or injury could leave you unable to make choices for yourself. Your advance directives give you a voice in medical treatment and name who can make healthcare decisions for you.

Are There Particular Forms to Fill Out?

Advance directives are written legal documents. Your physician or attorney can provide the forms and directions to complete them. You can also download forms from state government websites, AARP, the National Hospice and Palliative Care Organization (NHPCO), and the American Bar Association. If you move to a new state, ensure your current directives meet your new state's legal requirements.

Should I Hire a Lawyer to Create These Documents?

While many people work closely with their lawyers to create estate plan documents, you don't need an attorney to execute your medical directives. If your health or family situation is complicated, consult with your physician and attorney to address questions or concerns that arise as you draft paperwork.

What Happens If I Become Incapacitated Before I Complete Medical Directives?

If you're deemed incapacitated or incompetent and need medical care, your physician discusses treatment decisions with a close family member, based on who can make judgments on your behalf according to state law. A spouse, parent, adult child, or sibling will usually be called on to represent your best interests. If no family member is available or willing, a close friend or court-appointed guardian may fill this role.

AS YOU COMPLETE YOUR
MEDICAL DIRECTIVES

Don't be surprised if more issues or concerns arise as you fill out the information in the directives. Many of your questions may now focus on the involvement of others in your healthcare.

Will Doctors and My Healthcare Agent Follow My Directives?

If you want your physician, agent, and family to follow your directives:

- Share your healthcare wishes with them before any medical crisis happens.
- Ask if they're willing to abide by your decisions.
- Change physicians if your healthcare provider objects to treatment choices you've made.
- Avoid placing a loved one in a position going against their beliefs and values.

Will My Quality of Care Be Affected If I Have Directives in Place?

Remember, your directive goes into place only under specific conditions such as being in the late stage of a terminal illness or a permanent coma. When you're having a routine procedure, or your diagnosis is not life-threatening, advance directives don't play a role in your medical treatment.

What If I Have a Close Relative Who I Don't Want to Make Any of My Medical Decisions?

When you don't want a relative making healthcare choices for you, create a directive clearly naming someone else as your healthcare agent. Name a secondary agent too, in case your primary agent isn't available or able to fulfill the role. Ensure the people you trust with your medical wishes understand and agree to carry them out if called upon to do so.

Should I Create a Second Set of Medical Directives If I Live in a Different State for Part of the Year?

While many states will honor advance directives from another state, you should investigate the legal requirements for these documents in any state where you reside. Protect yourself and loved ones by having legally recognized forms in each state of residence.

AFTER COMPLETING
MEDICAL DIRECTIVES

Now that your directives are done, keep in mind that you'll likely need to revise your directives as you age and your family and health circumstances change.

Will First Responders Follow My Medical Directives If 911 Is Called?

First responders must provide medical care and transport to a hospital with some exceptions. They may not act if you're gravely ill, extremely elderly and frail, or have signed out-of-hospital Do Not Resuscitate (DNR) or "portable" clinician orders regarding life-sustaining treatment. If you're unable to communicate your wishes upon arriving at a hospital and you meet the conditions for the use of your advance directive, doctors and your healthcare agent will determine a course of treatment.

Where Should I Store My Medical Directives, and Who Should Have Copies?

While security is essential, placing your advance directive in a locked cabinet or a safe deposit box at a bank may prevent it from being used during a medical crisis. Keep original documents in a location where close relatives or friends can quickly access them if needed. You, a spouse, or a loved one may also carry a copy when you have a severe illness. Your doctor, primary and secondary healthcare agents, and local hospital should also have copies of your advance directives.

When Should I Revise My Medical Directives?

To ensure your documents still reflect your wishes, review them every few years. Revise your directives if health or circumstances change. If you're diagnosed with a serious condition or change your healthcare wishes, update your advance directive. Also, if you marry or divorce or your named health agent dies, revisit these critical legal documents.

Can I Revoke My Medical Directives?

You always have the right to make changes to your advance directives or revoke existing documents when legally competent. Just be sure to inform your physician, family members, and healthcare agents of the changes you adopt. Create new directives reflecting medical desires and provide everyone involved in your care with copies.

PLANNING FOR LONG-TERM CARE

Anticipating Needs and Covering the Costs

When you think about long-term care (LTC), you might envision an elderly relative in a nursing home. But LTC covers a continuation of services supporting an individual's personal or medical needs over some period—from months to years. Don't make the mistake of thinking LTC is just for the senior crowd. Younger adults with severe, chronic, or progressive medical conditions are a growing percentage of residents in long-term care settings.

According to the Department of Health and Human Services, the average amount of time people need LTC service is three years. Approximately 70 percent of adults age sixty-five today will need LTC support in the future, with 20 percent needing five or more years of care. Women also need to anticipate spending more on LTC because of longer life expectancies.

To create a strategy addressing potential care needs, you'll want to understand the different types and locations of LTC services providers. You also need to consider various costs relating to LTC and how to fund your plan.

LEVELS OF CARE, WHO PROVIDES IT, AND WHERE IT TAKES PLACE

Three levels of LTC services include custodial, intermediate, and nursing home care. Personal and medical needs determine the level of care services you receive. While preserving as much of a person's independence as possible, LTC services focus on maintaining a person's health and safety.

Custodial Care

To function independently, you must perform activities of daily living (ADLs) such as eating, bathing, and mobility without assistance. When you cannot, you'll need some level of personal care. If you need help bathing, dressing, toileting, organizing medicines, and getting to appointments, nonmedical custodial care is necessary to help you be healthy and safe.

Custodial care services can be provided by any family member or caregiver because there's no medical training or license requirement. This level of care can be given at home or in an assisted living or nursing home facility.

Intermediate Care

While there isn't a strict definition of *intermediate* care and service levels can vary, you can think of it as a combination of custodial and noncontinuous nursing care. Medical services are not the focus. Physician's orders guide nursing or rehabilitative services you might receive when needing an intermediate level of long-term care.

Daily personal assistance, along with nursing supervision and support focusing on prevention and rehabilitation, can help extend the time before you enter full-time nursing care. Those providing intermediate care may be a combination of family members, aides, therapists, and nurses. It can occur at home, in an ICF (intermediate care facility), or an assisted living setting.

Skilled Nursing Facilities

You may be discharged from a hospital to a skilled nursing facility (SNF) for short-term medical treatment or rehabilitation following a surgery or a severe medical event such as a stroke. While some SNFs are stand-alone, many are associated with long-term care facilities providing continuity of care.

Professional Nursing Care

When you require "around-the-clock" supervision and ongoing medical attention, you need indefinite custodial care and professional nursing services. Under your doctor's direction, nurses, therapists, social workers, and nurses' aides provide this highest LTC level.

It's possible to have this type of care in your home. But it can be challenging to find and coordinate the schedules of professional staff. Also, most people cannot afford to pay for twenty-four-hour care for a long period. When you need constant monitoring and access to skilled nursing services, a nursing home placement is generally required.

LONG-TERM CARE COSTS AND FUNDING YOUR LTC

You want to know what future LTC costs may be so you can design a plan to pay for them. But there's no crystal ball to help us see our future or anticipate increases in LTC costs. Our best option is to use our health status, family medical history, longevity information, and recent LTC research to help predict and plan for future expenses.

Most people prefer to "age in place" in their own homes for as long as possible. LTC in this setting is usually custodial and provided by paid or unpaid family members and friends or hired home healthcare aides. Depending on where you live, the average hourly wage of home health aides is between $11 and $21. Adult daycare centers providing custodial support for those aging at home averages around $75 a day.

Depending on the services you require, location and size of the facility, and amenities offered, the cost of residing in an assisted living community currently averages over $4,000 a month. Nursing home costs also vary widely but now average a staggering $7,500–$8,500 a month with an average stay of over two years.

As you consider the extensive costs for LTC, it's easy to see why it's crucial to plan. You won't have an estate to pass on to your heirs if you need care long-term and haven't established a way to pay for it.

Many have mistakenly thought LTC in nursing homes is entirely covered by regular health insurance or Medicare. It isn't. You may have to pay up to 100 percent of custodial nursing home care. Ways to privately finance LTC include personal savings, retirement funds, pensions, Social Security benefits, or equity from the sale of your home.

Long-Term Care Insurance

Purchasing long-term care insurance (LTCI) is another way to help finance future costs for various LTC services. If you qualify for coverage, premiums could range from $200–$500 a month or more, depending on the daily benefit you choose, your age, and your gender. LTCI is a complex product and is not an affordable or applicable option for many people.

There are alternatives to LTCI, including life insurance hybrid plans, long-term care annuities, and short-term-care policies. If you consider LTCI or any other options, talk with a financial professional about how the product aligns with your income, wealth building, and overall estate strategy.

Medicaid

When you have little to no savings, a limited income, or if you've spent down your assets, you'll likely rely on Medicaid to pay for your care long term. Eligibility rules vary from state to state. It's crucial to understand asset transfer rules and the "look back" period (typically five years) that can impact your Medicaid eligibility.

Veterans may also be able to access benefits to help pay for nursing home care. To find out more about LTC and your eligibility for VA benefits, contact your VA social worker.

DOCUMENTING END-OF-LIFE WISHES

A Final Gift to Your Loved Ones

Detailing end-of-life wishes in a funeral plan is an essential step in estate planning. As you consider mortality, you'll need to decide what you want to happen when you pass away. You aren't just taking care of yourself when you make a funeral plan. You're removing the burden on loved ones to decide what type of funeral arrangements you would've wanted. Instead of hoping to fulfill your final wishes, your prearranged plan allows them to focus on celebrating your life and memories of times together.

To complete a funeral plan, you need to choose what happens to your body upon death. You'll also decide the location of your final resting place, how you want to be memorialized, and how to notify others of your passing.

Some people decide on a traditional plan with an open casket, calling hours, a religious service, cemetery burial, and an obituary in a local paper. Others opt to be cremated and have a small, private memorial service with no public announcement. As long as it's done in advance, you get to decide on your final arrangements. Create a plan that aligns with your values and beliefs and that supports those who matter most to you.

THE DISPOSITION OF YOUR BODY

The idea of disposing of your body may seem cold or harsh. But after you're pronounced dead by a medical professional, your physical body needs attention. Your closest relatives or DPOA for healthcare will be asked to decide what happens to your body if you don't have a funeral plan.

A home viewing or funeral before your cremation or burial may be an option depending on where you live. While it isn't for everyone, a growing number of people are challenging the norms of typical funerals for cultural, economic, and environmental reasons.

If you opt for traditional after-death care, the chosen funeral home will be contacted to pick up your body and prepare it for viewing and services. Some funeral homes also offer cremations, so your remains may be transported to the same facility if that's your choice of disposition.

A direct cremation is an option when you desire to be cremated soon after death and before a funeral service or memorial gathering. Your body will be taken directly to a crematorium from your place of death. A family member or designated agent will meet with the director to sign any necessary consent documents, and your remains will be returned to them after cremation.

You'll be pre-enrolled to make an anatomical gift to the medical school if you decide to donate your body for medical research. Loved ones or designated agents should follow the medical school's directions on who to immediately contact after you pass. Medical school protocols will determine if your family or agent is in charge of arranging your body's transportation or if school representatives complete the transfer.

YOUR FINAL RESTING PLACE

To arrange a traditional funeral and burial, you need to choose a cemetery, burial plot, and a headstone or marker. A mausoleum is another option for the interment of your remains.

Family members can also take possession of your cremated ashes. If your remains aren't being interred at a cemetery, discuss what you'd like done with them. Make sure family members are comfortable with the ideas, such as keeping your ashes or scattering them in a memorable place. If they show concern, you may want a close friend as your agent to take possession—if they're willing to follow your wishes.

Natural or Green Burials

If you're interested in reducing your impact on the environment, consider a natural or green burial. States have various rules and regulations about the disposition of human remains. Still, it may be possible to be buried in an eco-friendly, biodegradable container without being embalmed.

ALLOWING OTHERS TO MEMORIALIZE YOU

Even if you have no interest in a funeral or memorial service, it's important to remember, this isn't just about you. It's also about your loved ones and close friends. Providing a time and place for people to gather to honor and remember you is an integral part of their grieving process.

Your religious and cultural beliefs may determine the type of end-of-life service you want and its location. A simple memorial service is what some people prefer after visiting hours. Others want their family and friends to informally gather and share a meal and great memories after some time has passed.

If forgoing any service is part of your funeral planning, discuss it with those closest to you, and explain your reasoning. Loved ones are more likely to honor your intentions when they understand why you don't want to be memorialized in a certain way.

YOUR OBITUARY OR DEATH NOTICE

There's no legal requirement to post an obituary notice. But you should talk to loved ones about whether an obituary or death notice is appropriate to announce your passing. Your age, the circumstances of death, and other personal matters may influence your decision.

It might surprise you that publishing a printed obituary can cost hundreds of dollars. The cost varies depending on the notice's length, whether you include a picture, the number of days the obituary is running, and the specific publication. Local newspapers often have an online option for obituaries at a much lower cost.

Some people prefer to have a close family member contact other relatives and friends rather than publish a local paper notice. Others post an obituary on a funeral home's website. Your death may also be announced by someone on social media whether you wanted that to happen or not.

FUNDING YOUR FINAL CARE

So You Can Rest in (Financial) Peace

You've considered the disposition options for your remains and ways for loved ones and friends to memorialize your life. Now it's time to figure out how to pay for your final care. Costs will vary greatly depending on the preparations chosen. But there are plenty of ways to fund arrangements so your family can grieve without worrying about financing your funeral.

COSTS

The average cost of a funeral and burial is $7,000–$10,000, depending on where you live and your choices for end-of-life care and celebrations. While money can be saved choosing cremation and simplifying the final arrangements, a full funeral service and cemetery expenses routinely run over $15,000 in some parts of the country.

Since your final expenses may reach a five-figure sum, it's essential to look at the pros and cons of different savings or payment options. Keep in mind, the funeral home you work with may expect full or partial payment before providing services. This may impact which option you choose to fund your final care.

Savings Account

One of the easiest ways to set aside money to cover final expenses is to open and fund a savings account. To bypass probate court, consider a joint account with rights of survivorship or a payable on death

(POD) account so that funds are available at the time of your passing for immediate use in paying for your funeral costs.

One disadvantage of a joint account is that the co-owner can access all the account's funds before you're deceased. While you may open a joint account with someone you trust, there's always a chance they could use the money in savings for a purpose you didn't intend. With a POD account, you generally cannot name an alternate beneficiary. This is a drawback if your beneficiary dies before you, because your account will end up in your estate and be subject to probate proceedings.

Keep It Simple and Save

For a simple and affordable funeral service, consider joining a local nonprofit memorial society for a low one-time membership fee (typically $35–$50). Focusing on preplanning one's final arrangements, these organizations educate members about end-of-life situations and significantly reduce their typical funeral costs.

Life Insurance

You may be thinking that your loved ones can use some of the proceeds of your life insurance policy to pay for your funeral when you pass away. But don't forget, you likely took out the policy to replace lost income and cover other expenses. Your family may face financial hardship if they need to use a significant portion of a basic life insurance policy to pay for your funeral.

While more than 50 percent of adults in the United States report holding a life insurance policy, almost half of insured policyholders have $100,000 of coverage or less. And group life insurance benefits offered free through an employer may provide only $25,000 to $50,000 of coverage.

Financial professionals suggest having a policy for at least 10x–15x your annual income. But if you have significant debt, children, or a dependent with special needs, you may need much more than that.

If you don't have a different plan to pay for your funeral, consider that expense as well when you increase your coverage or purchase a supplemental life insurance policy.

Burial or Final Expense Insurance

Another type of policy you can purchase is burial or final expense insurance. This small premium-based insurance policy typically provides $5,000 to $25,000 of coverage. After you're deceased, your beneficiary receives a payout they can use to cover any of your death-related costs.

While it may look like a good option to pay for your funeral, there are several drawbacks to burial insurance. Expensive premiums are the norm because medical exams are rarely required. You may pay more in premiums to maintain coverage than the insurance will pay out, and you can lose coverage if you miss premium payments. There's also no requirement that beneficiaries use your burial insurance payout to pay for your final costs. For these reasons, this type of insurance is not recommended unless you have no other options to consider.

Prepaid Funeral Contracts

You may opt to take care of as many of your final affairs as possible and prepay your funeral costs. A prepaid funeral contract can offer you peace of mind. Your heirs won't face the added stress of paying for your funeral during an already difficult time.

Insurance policies and funeral trust plans are what fund most prepaid funerals. Pre-need funeral insurance policies cover the future cost of predetermined final expenses. You make payments directly to an insurance company. Your funeral service provider collects payment after your death as the beneficiary of the policy. If you choose a funeral trust plan, you pay the funeral home director to create a trust account. The director then collects payment from the trust after your death.

Some people choose pre-need funeral contracts because they may not be counted as assets for Medicaid eligibility. Medicaid covers long-term care services for eligible recipients, but you must have limited income and assets to qualify.

Then again, there are plenty of reasons to pause before deciding a prepaid contract is right for you. These plans offer little protection if the insurer or funeral service provider declares bankruptcy or goes out of business. Your plan may also not be transferable or refundable if you relocate or change your mind about any funeral plans.

Veteran's Benefits

If you're a veteran, your spouse or beneficiaries are likely to qualify for partial reimbursement for your burial expenses. The Department of Veterans Affairs (VA) may fund other funeral-related expenses as well.

Be sure you understand the benefits surviving relatives should receive after you pass before creating a plan to fund your final care. They may not receive full reimbursement for all your final expenses. Still, you can protect loved ones by devising a strategy to save or pay for costs not covered by your government benefit.

Chapter 4

Taking Care of Others

Now that you have your "oxygen mask" on by taking care of your essential needs and estate planning documents in Chapter 3, it's time to focus on those you care about. You may have put off creating a will for a variety of reasons. But if you're waiting until your hair turns gray, your bank account hits seven figures, or your doctor says it's time, get past that thinking. It might help to look beyond the fact that a will relates to your death. Instead of viewing a will in terms of everything you'll lose, view it as a gift to those you love. Your will is the third essential element of an estate plan and the one that helps you take care of others when you no longer can.

WHY YOU NEED A WILL

Putting Your Final Wishes on Paper

You know your life will end someday. But you have plenty of company if you haven't started preparing for it yet. Many people procrastinate estate planning because of having to think about their death. While it's an emotional task, creating a valid will provides freedom from worry that your last wishes are communicated and carried out when you pass away.

If you die before making a will, your desires may not be known or followed. Instead, state intestacy laws determine who inherits your assets. That's why it's essential to understand the elements of a valid will so you can create one for the court to use in settling your estate.

WHAT A WILL IS AND WHAT IT INCLUDES

A will is a legal document directing the distribution of assets after your passing. Your will aids you in making your wishes known. But in reality, it is more helpful for those left behind.

The Who

The person creating a will is called the testator. In your will, you name a personal representative, sometimes referred to as an executor, and an alternate to manage your estate. A list of heirs and the naming of guardians for minor children are also a part of your will.

The What

To leave an heirloom necklace to a niece, your house to a brother, or your car to a favorite charity, you'll designate them as beneficiaries to that property in your will. You can also provide special instructions for your representative detailing how and when to distribute assets you're gifting to heirs.

You won't include all assets in your will because some directly transfer to named beneficiaries after your death. If you have bank accounts, life insurance, or an IRA, you probably designated beneficiaries when you opened the account or bought policies.

ESSENTIALS OF A WILL

A will has standard requirements, and to be valid, it must follow the laws of your state. In general, when creating a will, you must:

- Be of legal age to make a will (eighteen or older), married, or a member of the US Armed Forces.
- Be of sound mind, with the mental capacity and intent to understand you're creating a legally binding document to dispose of your property and assets.
- In writing, state you're of sound mind and body and list your personal property and to whom you're leaving it.
- Voluntarily, without being pressured or threatened, enter into and sign the will, witnessed by two parties with no interest in your estate.

Residuary Clause

Any assets or possessions not clearly named to someone in your will become part of the residuary estate. Those, along with any unclaimed assets remaining after all distributions, debts, final expenses, and tax payments, can be assigned to a beneficiary of choice through a residuary clause.

WITH OR WITHOUT A WILL, THERE'S PROBATE

Whether you have a will or not when you die, your estate's settlement is done through a probate court. As mentioned in Chapter 2, probate eventually becomes public record after your estate's settled.

What the Court Does

If you leave a will when you die, this is known as dying testate. The job of the probate court is to determine the validity of your will. Once presented to the court, a judge orders your estate's opening and formally appoints the personal representative. The judge oversees and works with your representative to pay off final debts, sell or distribute assets to beneficiaries and heirs, and ensure guardians take responsibility for your children.

If someone challenges your will, the probate court hears the case, settles disputes, and determines who receives what.

Intestacy: Dying Without a Will

When you lack a will at death, you're said to be intestate. Since you don't have a named representative, a probate judge chooses an administrator to manage your estate. The probate judge also decides on guardianship for minor children. Your state's intestate succession laws determine how assets are distributed to heirs. The administrator of your estate must follow the state's legal plan or formula for the distribution of property in the event of intestacy.

Failing to create a valid will means the people you want to receive your possessions may never get them. It also means someone you might not have chosen may end up raising your kids.

The Distribution of Property When There's No Will

While they vary by state, intestate succession laws are similar. If you die without a will, your relatives will generally inherit assets in the following order: your surviving spouse, children, grandchildren, parents, siblings, nieces or nephews, and grandparents.

Your Assets and Probate

As explained in Chapter 2, certain assets are not subject to the probating process. It's possible to bypass probate when you properly name beneficiaries on life insurance policies, trusts, and investment or retirement accounts. This results in a quicker distribution of assets and money savings by avoiding various legal fees.

Jointly owned assets and real property transfer to the surviving owner through a right of survivorship. Payable on death (POD) and transferable on death (TOD) accounts such as bank and brokerage accounts or individual stocks and bonds also avoid probate. These assets are re-registered to the new owners after providing a death certificate.

Personal possessions of value and property solely in your name—such as a car or home—need to go through probate. By having a will, you're able to decide who receives those assets. Without one, you're leaving the decision to others.

WHO NEEDS A WILL
(AND WHO MIGHT NOT)

You might delay creating a will when you're single, childless, and lack tangible assets. But a will should be a top priority if you're married or in a committed relationship, have kids, or own any property or possessions of value.

You don't want to make assumptions about what happens after you die. You need a will to be sure the people you love receive the things you plan to leave them, your possessions are divided up fairly, and the best choices are made about who'll care for your children.

Without a will, those you care most about may not have any right to make those decisions. Even when the court grants a loved one decision-making rights, hurt feelings and family conflict can arise without clear direction and guidance from your last will and testament.

Thinking about death and what may happen afterward can be uncomfortable. But avoiding it can cause increased stress for you and your family. Detail your final wishes in a valid legal form so you can take comfort in knowing everyone's cared for.

TYPES OF WILLS

From Basic to Last Minute

Now that you understand more about wills and the importance of drafting one, let's look at different types of wills and their pros and cons. The size of your estate and present life situation can impact your choice of wills. You may DIY a simple will to start an estate plan but hire an attorney to prepare a different type when your assets and family grow.

LAST WILL AND TESTAMENT

A last will and testament is the kind of document most people envision when they think about wills. In these, you record how you want your assets distributed after you're deceased. You can also designate beneficiaries, including family members, friends, or charitable organizations. You'll select someone to care for minor children and name a representative to ensure all obligations are met and conditions are followed.

Your last will and testament is a central piece of an overall estate plan. However, it does have some downsides. Wills must undergo probate, and those proceedings are not private. Probating a will can also take months, which means loved ones might have to wait a long time before receiving your assets.

If you prepare your will incorrectly, it could be declared invalid and disregarded by the court. Interested parties may also challenge your will. To prevent mistakes when creating a will, consider working with an experienced estate planning attorney.

Testamentary Trust

The option to add a testamentary trust to your will is something you might want to consider. Unlike other trusts, a testamentary trust does not go into effect until after your death. And since it's a part of your will, it must go through probate. You can use it to distribute a portion of assets or your entire estate to beneficiaries. Creating multiple testamentary trusts is also a possibility.

A testamentary trust might be useful when you want certain assets held until a specific time or event. For example, one might make sense if you want your child to wait to receive assets until after graduating from college or reaching age twenty-five. If the beneficiary of your testamentary trust must wait to achieve a milestone before receiving their inheritance, the trustee will need to report to the probate court each year until the assets' distribution is complete. Be aware this can lead to an increase in probate costs as the years go by, eating away at your estate's value. (We talk more about trusts in Chapter 5.)

SIMPLE WILL

You can create a simple or basic will to determine who receives assets, name a representative, and appoint a guardian for children. These are "no-frills" wills you can complete on state-specific legal forms or by using online service providers. Simple wills are generally appropriate only if you have a modest estate without many valuable assets to leave behind. The last will and testament is a better choice when you have complex assets, a blended family, or believe someone may contest your will.

Contesting a Will

People contest wills when they feel unfairly treated or excluded from receiving a share of an estate. But it usually takes an attorney with the right evidence to convince a court a will was incomplete or the testator was incompetent when writing it, or to find another legal reason that challenges its validity.

JOINT WILL

With a joint will, you and another person draft and sign a legal document agreeing to leave all your assets to each other. Typically, this document is created by spouses or committed partners who want the other person to inherit their estate after one of them dies. Once the second person dies, the estate's assets pass to beneficiaries jointly named by both spouses or partners.

Some couples choose to draft joint wills to save money and time. However, this can create several problems. When one person dies, their surviving partner cannot change the terms of the joint will. If the second person remarries, they cannot leave anything listed in the joint will to later-born children, stepchildren, or the new spouse or partner.

RECIPROCAL OR MUTUAL WILL

A reciprocal or mutual will may be a better option than a joint will. This type of estate planning document includes two nearly identical wills. However, each will is signed individually. In a reciprocal will, each member of the couple can state that their surviving partner is to inherit the entire estate and include different details. A reciprocal will might also allow someone other than the surviving partner to receive a portion of the estate.

For example, partners can include provisions for children from prior relationships to inherit some assets. If you choose to create a mutual will as a couple, be sure to name back-up beneficiaries you both agree on in your separate paperwork. This can help prevent family disputes if both of you pass away at the same time.

HOLOGRAPHIC, NUNCUPATIVE, AND DEATHBED WILLS

While these wills are not standard, we mention them because they're poor estate planning options. A holographic will is handwritten by a person who believes they might not survive a dangerous situation. For example, a soldier deployed to a combat zone might create a holographic will. However, not all states recognize holographic wills. Even in states accepting handwritten wills, they're likely to be challenged in court.

A nuncupative will is an oral will in which a person speaks their final wishes instead of writing them down. In most cases, someone creates a nuncupative will when they're terminally ill and likely to die soon. As with holographic wills, not every state acknowledges nuncupative wills, and the rules for them may differ in states where they're recognized.

A deathbed or last-minute will is just like it sounds: something created when someone is dying. It's usually a handwritten or typed document. Still, no matter how a deathbed will is made, it might not withstand a challenge. If the court deems it invalid, they can disregard your wishes, and assets will pass under state intestacy laws.

NAMING A PERSONAL REPRESENTATIVE

Being Trustworthy Is a Must, but Just the Beginning

As touched on earlier, you'll be naming specific individuals in your will to manage your estate, look after minor children, and receive assets. For some of you, choosing these individuals is easy; for others, not so much. Either way, we'll help you determine who you must name in your will and who you should. Let's first discuss your personal representative.

DETERMINING PERSONAL REPRESENTATIVES

Naming a personal representative means giving someone the legal authority to handle your estate when you're gone. The individual you name will have the fiduciary responsibility of wrapping up your legal and financial affairs in the best interests of your estate and beneficiaries. Duties of a representative include:

- Filing your will with the probate court and representing your estate
- Notifying agencies and financial companies of your death
- Paying final bills and settling outstanding loans
- Ensuring payment of income, estate, or inheritance taxes due
- Maintaining, selling, distributing, or disposing of property within your estate

Your person of choice should be the family member or friend you trust most, who's also willing and able to assume the role. While choosing one individual to serve as your representative keeps things simple, opting for two or more representatives could be beneficial in some situations. Additionally, while it's not a requirement, we suggest you choose at least one substitute (alternate) to assume the position if your representative is unable or unwilling to do so when the time comes.

Considerations When Choosing a Personal Representative

Depending on the size of your estate and the activities involved to settle it, a representative may spend a great deal of time managing your affairs and interacting with heirs and beneficiaries over several months (or years). Besides trustworthiness, you'll want to consider other characteristics of potential representatives before making a final selection.

Bonding

A surety bond (aka probate, personal representative, estate, or fiduciary bond) in estate planning is an agreement between three parties: the insurance company, the estate's representative, and the estate. It's designed to protect beneficiaries from the negligent or fraudulent acts of the personal representative.

---

1. **How responsible are they?** Someone who doesn't have a high degree of integrity in their life matters will not all of a sudden have one for yours.
2. **Are they savvy about personal finance and have their financial affairs in order?** This is important for a few reasons. One is that they could be selling property, negotiating bills, handling taxes, and other financial matters. Another is for bonding purposes. If

they're deemed a financial risk and are unable to secure a bond, the court may not allow them to serve as your representative.

3. **Are they patient, caring, and sensible?** Your representative will need availability to perform the role and be patient when it comes to time-consuming matters and people. You'll want someone who exhibits care about the work they're doing and for those involved in your estate. They'll also need to be fair and sensible and not let emotions and beneficiaries cloud their judgment.

4. **Would the courts allow them to serve?** Minors are not allowed to serve as a representative. Non-US citizens or ex-felons are usually disqualified or at least unable to be the sole representative.

5. **Could their age or lifestyle be a factor?** When you're thirty, choosing someone twenty years older as your representative might not be an issue, but when you're fifty, it could be. Naming a substitute representative is always a wise choice. It's more critical when you name someone who's older or has a high-risk career or lifestyle.

6. **Do they live near or reasonably close to you?** A representative who's not local may find it more time-consuming and challenging to manage your estate from a distance. It typically won't make much difference in simple estates. Yet, more complex ones could face settlement delays when your representative is across (or out of) the country.

7. **Do they get along with, or are they respected by, your family?** A difficult representative who causes drama or lacks respect among most family members is someone you should probably avoid. When you feel you don't have another choice, consider naming a co-representative to help resolve potential conflicts.

Once you've settled on potential representatives and substitutes, speak with them to see if they're willing to take on the role before making your final decisions and listing them in your will. Even if you choose to pay them, you might find people are reluctant to take on the job.

When you don't have someone willing or capable of assuming the responsibility, you might select an accountant, attorney, bank, or other institution to serve as your representative.

Could Hiring a Professional Representative Make Sense?

If your estate is large or complicated due to its types of assets or your family's size and dynamics, hiring a professional representative could be a smart move. While it's going to cost you, it may be money well spent if your estate needs more time and attention or you don't have someone in your life suitable for the role. Also, hiring a professional representative can remove the significant responsibility from a loved one who's grieving your loss.

Hiring a professional could also mean your estate settles quickly because they're knowledgeable and experienced with the job's financial and legal requirements. Just keep in mind, the more complex your estate, the more time and cost it may take to settle.

Professionals could charge a fee based on the hours they work or a percentage (1–5 percent, typically) of your estate's total value. Total costs will vary, of course. If the price is a big concern, you may reduce some fees by hiring a professional to work with a personal representative. The professional can direct the settlement of your estate while your representative takes on the minor tasks. Before deciding on a firm or professional, be sure they have the particular expertise your estate will need. Also, be clear on how your estate will be charged for services.

You shouldn't rush to name a representative. But don't let deciding on one hold up the process of creating your will.

WHEN MINOR CHILDREN ARE INVOLVED

Protecting the Kids

Kids are an awesome responsibility: precious, sometimes frustrating, and one of the most amazing wonders in life. As parents or other important people in their lives, we assume many responsibilities, such as providing love, time, attention, and sharing our values and knowledge. Protecting and providing for their economic needs is also top of the list.

Whether you have your own kids to protect and provide for; serve as a guardian of someone else's children; or want to include nieces, nephews, or grandchildren in your estate plan, this section is for you. It covers ensuring for a minor's care in the event of your death and how to leave assets behind for them.

NAMING GUARDIANS

Thinking about naming a guardian(s) for your children might bring tears to your eyes. The thought of not being here to care for them and watch them grow is heart-wrenching. But it's also extremely important to be sure you have a say in who would step into the guardianship role if you and their other parent cannot care for them. Procrastinating on the decision could mean someone you wouldn't choose could be legally assigned the role. The court generally appoints a close family member as guardian when there's no surviving (or fit) parent. Yet, you can't be sure who they'll select if you don't name someone yourself.

Considerations When Choosing Guardians

Like traits you want in a personal representative, a guardian for your kids should be trustworthy, patient, caring, sensible, and local. Consider someone who chooses a healthy lifestyle and has positive relationships with family and friends. You'll obviously want someone loving and capable of providing the structure and emotional support your child would need. A person with similar values and beliefs could make a good choice.

If you have more than one minor, your decision may be more involved. In some cases, you may need to decide if having more than one guardian makes sense. Also, if you have a child with special needs, there could be more for you to consider depending on the care your child requires. In any case, you'll want to pick a willing person who can best manage your children's emotional, physical, and fiscal care.

Common people to consider besides the other legal parent are grandparents, stepparents, older siblings, aunts, uncles, family friends, or even previous childcare providers. For an older child, neighbors or the parents of your child's friend could also be an option.

Once you've identified someone, discuss guardianship with them to see if they're willing to accept legal custody and responsibility for your child and their care if you pass away. Only name an individual in your will if they agree to the position. Courts generally prioritize your recommendation for guardianship unless someone challenges it with compelling evidence after your death.

Naming Someone to Manage Assets for Children

Secondary to naming a guardian for your child's care is naming someone to manage assets or life insurance proceeds you leave to them. Because minors can't make legal transactions on property over a certain amount (up to $5,000 depending on state laws), a legally responsible adult must be named to oversee it. The court will oversee the property guardian's management of the assets until they pass to your child at eighteen. This includes the use of assets for your child's regular care: their living, health, and educational expenses.

This "property guardian" (aka custodian, trustee, or property manager) can and probably should be the same person with guardian responsibilities. But it's a decision you'll want to think through.

Your spouse, or the child's other parent, are natural options for you to consider as a property guardian. Yet this isn't always the best or even an available choice depending on your circumstances. As with a custodial guardian, other options include close family members and friends. Naming a substitute property guardian is wise too.

LEAVING PROPERTY TO KIDS

You name someone to oversee your child's inherited property. Now how exactly should it be left to them and managed? And what do you do if you're not crazy about a young adult getting their hands on a large amount of money?

When leaving property to a minor child, you have a couple of options in addition to using a property guardian. You can use a custodian under the Uniform Transfers to Minors Act (UTMA) or set up a trust.

At a minimum, you'll name a property guardian, as discussed earlier. But there are some drawbacks to stopping there, including the court's substantial reporting requirements and regulations and the fact that assets are turned over to your child when they turn eighteen. When less court involvement is desired, the UTMA is a better option. When assets are substantial, or you want the property supervised until your child reaches a specific age, a trust may be the best option (discussed in Chapter 5).

The UTMA is available in every state except South Carolina and varies by the state concerning when your child's assets transfer. In most states, the transfer is at age twenty-one, but it could be eighteen, twenty-five, or thirty.

You'll list the property and the minor you're leaving it to and name a custodian (and a substitute) in your will. You'll also specify that the custodian is to act under the UTMA of your state, which gives them the rights to oversee, manage, and use assets for the benefit of your child. While no court supervision is required, proper records must be kept, and the custodian must act responsibly.

Children Conceived after a Parent's Death

The property rights of children conceived from the use of frozen sperm, eggs, or embryos after a person's death (known as posthumous conception) are a gray area and rapidly changing. You may need explicit language in estate planning documents providing your partner with the authority to make decisions regarding your frozen genetic material. Our best advice is to talk with your attorney about state laws that may exist and how to legally provide for posthumously conceived children in your estate plan.

Naming Minors As a Beneficiary (or Not) on Life Insurance

When children are minors, it makes sense that your estate may not be substantial enough to leave a large amount of property to them. In this case, securing a term life insurance policy to provide for their needs can be a logical choice. But insurance companies can't legally give minors the payout outright. You'll want to avoid naming them as a beneficiary (or contingent beneficiary) without naming a custodian under the UTMA or using a trust.

DETERMINING BENEFICIARIES AND INHERITANCES

Who Gets What

By now, you probably have a good idea of the beneficiaries you want to name in your will. If you haven't created a list yet, visit the "Who to Consider in Your Planning" section of Chapter 1 to get that task finished.

In Chapter 2, we discussed creating an inventory of your financial assets and significant property. Now's a good time to add other items to that list, including personal property and heirlooms.

PROPERTY THAT DOESN'T GO IN YOUR WILL

Generally, property that's transferred automatically to someone else through ownership rights isn't gifted in your will (see Chapter 6 for details). In other words, your will won't affect the following:

- Assets designated to someone through transfer on death (TOD) or payable on death (POD) accounts, deeds, or registrations
- Joint tenancy property
- Life insurance proceeds or retirement accounts with named beneficiaries
- Assets already promised to someone in a legal contract such as a prenuptial or partnership agreement
- Property in a living trust with designated beneficiaries

If a named beneficiary or joint tenancy owner passes away before or at the same time as you, the residuary clause in your will assigns a new heir to inherit those assets unable to be distributed through the methods listed previously.

WHO GETS WHAT

With your prepared lists of beneficiaries and all the property you own, you can begin making decisions about how to divide up your assets. Certain choices will seem obvious, and you'll arrive at others through logic or sentiment. But inheritance decisions may be more difficult if you have an heir with a disability, challenging family circumstances, or a complex estate.

Should you treat each beneficiary the same and give them equal inheritances or leave more to some heirs than others? Only you can answer that question for your estate. But keep in mind, what's fair isn't always equal.

An Equal Division of Assets

It makes sense that many people choose to divide up their property equally among their heirs. If you've treated them alike and they have similar needs and circumstances, there would be little reason to leave more to one person than another.

But you may have a different goal when you opt for this strategy: keeping the peace. Even if you'd prefer to divide things up differently, leaving each beneficiary the same inheritance avoids the appearance of favoritism. It may also head off serious family conflict over your estate.

An equal division of assets doesn't mean everything you own is sold, with proceeds being split evenly after your death (or your surviving spouse's). And you don't have to go through every one of your assets and assign them to beneficiaries when you draft a will.

A simpler method is to leave your heirs with equal percentages of your overall estate. This helps when assets you hold, and their fair market values, change over time.

For example, your home and its belongings, the cash in bank accounts, and your IRA may all be approximately the same value when you update your will. But by the time you pass away, your IRA and home value increase, but your cash is depleted from your long-term care expenses. If you left your home to your oldest child, the IRA to your middle child, and your youngest got the cash, what they ultimately receive is not likely what you intended. Plus, you could accidentally be disinheriting your youngest and inviting a challenge to your will.

Unequal Inheritances

It's important not to just default to leaving everyone the same inheritance. No one wants to create family disputes when they die, but do all your heirs have a right to inherit a portion of your estate? While your spouse and minor children generally have inheritance rights determined by your state of residence, you get to define what "fair" means when it comes to dividing up your property.

Here are some reasons people choose to leave a bigger slice of their estate "pie" to individual heirs. If you have one of the following situations, think carefully before making decisions to cut your pie unequally.

1. **Special needs dependent.** A family member with special needs will likely need more financial support than other heirs, even if they receive government benefits.

2. **Compensation for help.** When heirs provide primary care, they may deserve compensation for their efforts or to replace their lost income during that time.

3. **Balance prior support.** When an heir has received more financial support than others—a sizable down payment for a house or funds to start a business—giving other heirs a larger portion from estate assets can balance things out.

4. **Age of dependents.** If there's a significant age difference between children, a bigger portion of assets may be needed to provide for younger kids.

5. **Family business.** When some heirs are involved in the business and helped it grow or are interested in taking it over, they may be rewarded for those efforts.

6. **Blended family.** Some people leave smaller portions of their estate to stepchildren because they'll likely receive assets from another parent too.

7. **Perceived need.** Heirs with higher net worths may not need the same size inheritance.

8. **Relationship dynamics.** Strained relationships or estrangement from heirs may determine the percentage of assets left to them—if any inheritance is given at all.

It's Your Decision

You control what portion of your assets a beneficiary receives and when they receive it. A will provides an outright inheritance, while a trust can hold a beneficiary's inheritance for years. Consider the needs of your heirs when determining how best to pass on final gifts.

Depending on your situation, it can be a good idea to sit down with family members to discuss your will and how you intend to distribute assets. It may be a short conversation if you divide things equally. But it's a good time to explain why someone may receive a larger or smaller portion of your estate. If you aren't comfortable talking with family members about your decision, consider writing them a letter that's shared at the time of your death.

MINIMIZING CONFLICT

Plan for Family Peace

Even though your family may come together and grieve your loss, they may turn on each other when it comes time to discuss who gets what from your estate. There could be trouble if you already have challenging family circumstances, but even close families can have serious disputes and damage relationships over the settling of an estate.

You won't be around to answer questions or explain decisions you made about how you chose to distribute your assets. That's why it's essential to understand what causes disagreements between loved ones left behind so you can take proactive steps to plan for family peace.

REASONS FOR CONFLICT BETWEEN HEIRS

Every family situation is unique, but there are a number of common reasons for conflict when it comes to how your loved ones may communicate and behave when dealing with your estate.

1. **Acting without personal representative approval.** An heir may enter a deceased person's home to take belongings they want or believe have been left to them, and those on joint accounts may wrongly spend funds of the deceased. These types of actions cause suspicion and may even be considered theft of estate items.

2. **Ambiguous or outdated legal documents.** If your directives aren't clear or you fail to update a will or trust after major life events, your heirs may question or challenge the paperwork. An ex-spouse may be a beneficiary of estate assets, or you may accidentally disinherit someone by selling an investment you'd planned to leave for them.

3. **Poor communication.** Your representative or trustee may not share information with beneficiaries on a timely basis. When this happens, your loved ones may start suspecting the worst and assume their inheritance is in danger.

4. **Broken promises.** A beneficiary may be surprised to learn they are not receiving something you promised to leave them. This can cause hurt feelings and resentment toward other family members and leave the person in charge of your estate in a difficult position.

5. **Refusal to cooperate or compromise.** Whether it's co-representatives who can't agree on decisions or siblings who won't work together to maintain shared property left to them, it's difficult when people can't get along. Mediators or personal attorneys may even be needed to clear up these situations.

6. **Greed or entitlement.** Your heirs may be angry and want more or different assets from your estate. Some beneficiaries may believe they deserve a more generous portion or disagree with asset valuation. They might even disagree with your trustee receiving payment for all the work they do managing and distributing your assets.

Preventing inheritance disputes can save your beneficiaries time and money. More importantly, it can also help preserve their relationships. While you can't prevent all quarrels during the time it takes to settle your estate, there are plenty of things you can do to help calm emotions and make the process easier.

WAYS TO MINIMIZE CONFLICT

While there are plenty of reasons your loved ones may have disputes with one another over your estate, there are actions you can take to reduce family friction.

Predict Points of Conflict

In addition to giving careful consideration to how to split up your assets between beneficiaries, you also need to think about how your choices will affect them when you're gone. If you plan to disinherit a child or leave unequal shares of your estate to heirs, how will they react to that news? Heirs who feel left out or cheated may challenge your decisions. Make sure you don't leave your representative to deal with the issues you created.

Valuing Assets

Consider having jewelry, collections, antiques, or heirlooms appraised so your representative isn't challenged on their value. You should also have your family home appraised if it's being passed on to an heir as part of your estate.

Choose Fiduciaries Wisely

The people who'll be making decisions for you, managing your finances, and handling your estate need to be more than just people you trust. They also need to have the skills for the position, the availability to take on the responsibility, and the patience to work with everyone involved during an emotionally charged time. Keep in mind that a corporate fiduciary may provide the experience and unbiased administrative skills you need.

Communicate with Your Beneficiaries

Depending on your personal situation, it may make sense to call a family meeting to discuss your estate planning ideas before executing the documents. Talking openly with family members about your death may be uncomfortable. Still, it also models open and honest dialogue about a topic everyone eventually faces. You may decide to wait until after your plan is in place to share it with your heirs. While giving specific details isn't always necessary, letting them know you have a plan is essential. Should you not want to discuss your final wishes and inheritance decisions, you might write a letter to your beneficiaries instead. You can then decide if it's delivered while you're alive or after you pass away.

Create Valid Estate Planning Documents

If you rush to draft paperwork or try to DIY an elaborate plan, you may end up with invalid papers or language that won't withstand a challenge in court. Your legal forms need to be clear and as straightforward as possible while still accomplishing your estate planning goals. Your attorney will help you create documents that aren't open to interpretation. Once your plan is in place, don't forget to tell your heirs its location!

Review and Amend Your Plan

When you get married or divorced, celebrate the birth of a baby, or mourn the loss of a loved one, you need to update your estate planning documents. Even if there hasn't been a significant life change, you should still review your plan at least every few years. You want to keep it as current as possible so that you and your beneficiaries are protected. Chapter 8 goes into detail on when to amend your plan.

Set Expectations and Encourage Transparency

You may not realize the impact your words can have on your loved ones after you're gone. While communicating with your heirs about your plan is essential, telling them how you expect them to behave in your absence is necessary too. Encourage your loved ones to meet soon after your death to ask questions and share concerns about your estate and the timeline for settling it. You'll never know if your efforts to prevent family conflict pay off, but the impact may be felt for generations.

COMPLETING YOUR WILL (BUT CONTINUING TO PLAN)

Your Last Will and Testament Probably Isn't

When drafting a will, you'll ensure your property is inventoried and beneficiaries are designated to inherit your assets. You'll name a personal representative who's willing and able to settle your estate. Don't forget to include an alternate in case your designated representative is no longer living or is unable or unwilling to assume the role. If you have minor children, you'll choose a guardian to accept responsibility for their care and a property guardian to manage any assets you leave for them.

You also need to make sure property you don't want to go through probate doesn't. This means naming primary and contingent beneficiaries on life insurance policies, retirement accounts, and other financial accounts that allow them. It might also require establishing POD or TOD (payable on death or transferable on death) on bank accounts and other assets that don't name beneficiaries, such as savings and checking accounts and vehicles. Finally, you want to be certain jointly owned property is titled correctly. This means you must understand how it transfers upon your death according to the laws of your state.

IS PROBATE A CONCERN?

A will helps you have a say in who gets your assets upon your death and cares for your children if you die when they're minors. But a will can't help you avoid probate or taxes. It also won't keep your estate details private or prevent family conflicts. You'll need other estate planning tools and tactics to accomplish those things.

Before you worry too much about avoiding probate, let's review when it might be nothing to fear and when it may be the better choice for your estate.

Probate may not be a big concern when you:

- Plan to avoid probate from the beginning and title assets properly
- Name primary and contingent beneficiaries and keep them updated
- Stay diligent about reviewing and updating your estate planning documents
- Aren't worried about privacy
- Have a minimal estate

Additionally, because probate courts provide a means for resolving tricky estate matters, you may want probate when you have significant debts or own a business that's failing. This is because creditors have a limited time to make a claim against your estate.

If you're unsure if you need to take additional probate avoidance measures, speak with an estate planning attorney to determine your best option.

A FEW MORE STEPS

There are some additional steps to complete your will and this phase of your estate plan. These include writing letters of instruction to your representative and guardian. They also involve telling your family about your plan and storing it securely while making sure it's accessible to those who'll need it. These steps are detailed in Chapter 8, along with:

- Tips for writing letters to loved ones
- A list of mistakes to avoid
- Steps to creating an emergency binder
- Questions to help you further your legacy planning
- An estate planning checklist
- Information on when to update your estate plan

Keep Going

While you might be tempted to stop here because you've covered the essentials—a financial POA, advance directives, and a will—we encourage you to continue. Even if you're young and single, and have a small estate today, all of those things won't likely be true later in your life. Understanding how trusts work (Chapter 5), how taxes and financial gifts affect your estate annually and over time (Chapter 6), and what situations need more consideration (Chapter 7) can prove valuable later even if they are not relevant for you now. Plus, it can help you assist your family with their estate planning.

Covering All Your Bases

Some additional reminders and tips:

- You must sign your will in the presence of two legally competent witnesses to "execute" it.
- Many states require two people who don't benefit from your will to act as witnesses, but check state laws to understand any other requirements.

- A living will is not the same as a last will and testament. Make sure you understand the difference and obtain both crucial documents.

- A testamentary trust is not a living trust, and it doesn't avoid probate. Instead, a testamentary trust is part of your will, and it holds specific property for a particular purpose. It goes into effect during the probating process.

- If you own a vacation home or other property in a state different from your state of residency, your estate will also need to open probate in the additional state.

- While a will created in your home state is valid in other states, state laws and terminology vary. Your will may not perform as you intend it to in a state other than the one where it was prepared.

Revoking a Will

Because your will isn't acted upon until you die, it can typically be changed or canceled at any time before death as long as you are legally competent. You can make minor changes through a codicil, but creating a new will is the best option for making several changes. Note: In some states, when you receive a final decree of divorce, dissolution, or annulment, any gifts you made in a will to your now ex-spouse are automatically revoked. Still, it may be best to change your will to ensure your former spouse doesn't receive any assets they aren't entitled to.

Codicil

A codicil is a legally binding document amending an executed will. Two witnesses must sign it (not necessarily the same people used when executing the original will). A codicil should mention the date of the will it is amending and be kept with the original will.

To get rid of your first will completely, shredding it, tearing it up, burning it, or deleting electronic copies of it may not be enough. You'll want to cancel it (and any codicils to it) by inserting a clause in your newly created will, specifically stating all prior wills and codicils are revoked. If you don't, probating your estate can become very complicated if multiple wills are presented (this could happen if heirs have copies of prior wills). To ensure things turn out according to your latest wishes, revoke previous wills and destroy all originals and copies.

Continue Planning

Executing your will is a great accomplishment. With it, you're helping protect those you care about and distributing the assets you'll leave behind in a meaningful way. Give yourself a pat on the back! Now continue planning. As you grow your net worth and experience life events, you'll likely need to update paperwork and possibly add more tools to your estate planning toolbox. Don't let your hard work thus far be erased because you didn't make adjustments to your original plan when things changed. Continue to evaluate your goals as you age, adjust as necessary, and be confident your loved ones are taken care of and final wishes are followed.

Chapter 5

Is a Trust the Answer?

While most everyone needs a will, some people may also benefit from using a trust. Several different types of trusts can serve as an efficient way to transfer property upon death. They can also protect and control assets, reduce estate taxes, avoid probate, maintain privacy, and more. Trusts are not just for the wealthy, and they needn't be overly complicated. While they may have benefits you're looking for, the type of assets you own and your circumstances determine if they're a smart addition to your estate plan.

AN OVERVIEW OF TRUSTS

What They Are and Who's Involved

Before deciding if you should create a trust as part of your estate plan, it's essential to learn more about the basics of trusts and who manages and benefits from them. Since there are many different kinds, we'll introduce you to basic types of trusts.

WHAT IS A TRUST?

Have you ever asked a family member, friend, or neighbor to check on your home when you're away on vacation? If so, you made an agreement with someone you assume is trustworthy to oversee property on your behalf and for your benefit. That's a verbal trust.

In estate planning, most trusts are written legal arrangements involving three players. They are the creator of the trust (the trustor), the person or company who oversees it (the trustee), and those who benefit from it (beneficiaries). Depending on the type of trust you draft, you can serve in one, two, or all three trust roles.

Creating a trust gives you control over what property goes into the trust and who gets the assets and when. It may also offer asset protection and tax benefits. But the advantages vary depending on the type of trust and the positions you play in the trust.

The assets used to fund your trust and generate income for beneficiaries are called the trust principal (aka trust corpus). Personal belongings, cash, stocks, bonds, life insurance policies, homes and other real estate, and business assets are examples of property that fund a trust's principal. Depending on the type of trust, you may be able to contribute additional assets or remove property later. This results in changes to the principal amount.

Examples of income earned by a trust's principal include interest earned on bank accounts, stock dividends, net income from rental properties, or earnings from businesses owned by the trust.

Unlike a will, a trust goes into effect as soon as you create it. You can also direct assets to be distributed at different times with a trust—not just after your death. You may instruct the trust to provide assets to heirs before you die or at predetermined times in the future. A properly funded trust helps you avoid probate and protects your privacy since it doesn't become a public record.

As you keep reading, know there are several kinds of trusts that serve different functions, and there are dozens of other names for them. Since the specific requirements can vary, you'll need to make sure to understand the rules and laws for creating a valid trust in your state.

WHO'S INVOLVED IN A TRUST

We've introduced you to the three main parties involved in a trust: the trustor, trustee, and beneficiary. Now, we'll better define each role and introduce you to another key player: the successor trustee.

As the trustor (aka grantor, settlor, donor, or trust maker), you establish the trust and contribute assets to it. You also determine how the funds should be managed and name beneficiaries of the trust.

When you set up a trust, you'll appoint a trustee. This is you or another individual, group of people, or a company who agrees to over-see, manage, and distribute assets in a trust per your instructions. Your trustee has the fiduciary duty to take care of the property in the trust for the sole benefit of your beneficiaries. When more than one person serves in this role at the same time, they're called co-trustees. Large banks often have trust companies or departments to fill this position.

Fiduciary Duty

A fiduciary duty is a responsibility to do what's best for another person. By accepting a trusteeship, you're held to a high standard. You cannot put personal interests over those of beneficiaries. You must carry out the trustor's stated wishes, act transparently, and regularly communicate with beneficiaries.

As trustor, you'll also name a replacement (successor) trustee who steps into the role if your trustee is unwilling or unable to serve or becomes incapacitated or dies. People often list alternate trustees to make sure they always have a dependable individual managing their trust.

The persons or organizations who receive a financial benefit from the assets in your trust are your beneficiaries. Depending on how you allocate trust assets, you name beneficiaries as either principal or income beneficiaries. A principal beneficiary receives the principal property in the trust, and an income beneficiary receives income the principal trust property earns.

BASIC TYPES OF TRUSTS

Trusts are either inter vivos ("living" trusts) or testamentary ("death" trusts). Inter vivos trusts hold the property you place in the trust and are in effect while you're living. As mentioned in Chapter 4, a testamentary trust is part of your last will. It directs your representative to create a trust after your death during probate proceedings.

Revocable versus Irrevocable

There are two categories of living trusts: revocable and irrevocable. Even though a trust holds your property, you retain the right to amend or terminate a revocable trust as long as you're not deemed mentally incompetent.

With an irrevocable trust, you give up all ownership rights to the property you place into it, so you can only modify the trust under certain circumstances.

While you can change your will's testamentary trust section before death, a testamentary trust is considered irrevocable because it doesn't go into effect until after your death.

Simple or Complex

Trusts are also simple or complex. Simple trusts distribute all income produced by their principal each year to beneficiaries (but not charitable organizations) but retain all the trust's principal.

However, if the trust accumulates income, makes distributions to a charity, or distributes any of the principal, it's considered a complex trust and may be subject to high tax rates.

Trusts are essential estate planning tools for many people, not just those who have seven-figure net worths. We cover revocable, irrevocable, and other particular types of trusts in greater detail in later sections.

WHY YOUR ESTATE DOES (OR DOESN'T) NEED A TRUST

Many Pros to Them, but More Than Some Need

When you search for details about trusts and whether you should create one, you'll find lots of information. Advice will range from everyone needs one to avoid probate, to don't believe anyone who's telling you to make one. While these opposing views have valid points, deciding to form a trust in your estate plan depends on your specific situation and goals.

WHY YOU MIGHT ESTABLISH A TRUST

We already know those with large financial houses use estate planning tools such as trusts to protect their assets and heirs. But let's look at some of the reasons why you might consider creating one even as you're growing your net worth.

Minor Children

Think back to when you were graduating from high school. If you received a large inheritance when you were eighteen, what would you have done with it? Few young adults understand how to manage money—especially large amounts of it—or have the discipline necessary to make financial decisions to benefit their futures.

You can set up a trust to hold assets such as life insurance policies or investment accounts. If you pass away, a trust can direct a trustee to provide financial support to your minor (or young adult) child for whatever you deem appropriate, including medical bills, higher education, or wedding expenses. You can also direct when and how your adult child will receive direct disbursements from your trust. This prevents them from receiving a lump sum of money when they aren't prepared to handle it.

Blended Family

While you'd likely want to support your spouse financially when you pass away, it's also essential to think about how to protect your kids from a previous relationship. Without a trust, the beneficiaries who ultimately receive your assets might be those of your surviving spouse when they pass. And if your spouse gets remarried and dies before their new partner, the new partner and their kids may end up with your property.

An attorney can help you establish a trust to protect your children from being disinherited.

Unmarried Couple

Since an unmarried couple doesn't have the same rights as a married one, a partner may accidentally disinherit the other when they die. To keep the interests of both people safe, one tool life partners can use is a trust.

Your partner can serve as your successor trustee and manage your estate if you become incapacitated. They could also be named the beneficiary if you want to prevent intestacy laws from determining which of your heirs end up with your property. Placing an asset (i.e., home or car) into a trust allows for its transfer to your partner after your death.

Property in Different States

Suppose you own property in more than one state. In that case, your executor may have to deal with probate proceedings in each location after your death. One way to avoid this is by transferring ownership of the properties to your trust.

Your estate planning attorney makes sure the deed for out-of-state property is prepared correctly, recorded, and transferred into the trust. This helps to prevent issues when it's time for the distribution of trust assets.

Business Ownership

While some people decide to wait until they retire to create a trust, business owners can benefit from adding a trust to their estate plan while working. If something terrible happens, and you become incapacitated or pass away, you'll already have a plan. This allows your trustee and beneficiaries to take over and manage any financial and business dealings.

The type of business structure you have can affect the transfer of business interests into your trust. Talk with your attorney about business succession planning and the pros and cons of setting up a trust and titling your business assets in the trust's name.

Concerned about Declining Health

A trust may be a smart decision if you worry about how a decrease in physical or mental health might affect your ability to manage your assets.

Rather than a court appointing a conservator if you can no longer act on your behalf, a replacement trustee can take over the management of trust assets. Establishing a trust before an illness or disability allows you to maintain control, even when you can no longer actively care for property in your estate.

Challenging Family Dynamics

When you have difficult family circumstances, you may decide to create a trust because it offers more privacy than a will. A trust can also help support a spendthrift child or one addicted to alcohol, drugs, or gambling.

If you are estranged from any of your children, you can use a trust to include them as beneficiaries (possibly at a reduced percentage of assets or with stipulations they must meet before receiving assets) or disinherit them.

While a child who doesn't have a relationship with a parent can still contest a parent's trust, it may be more difficult to successfully challenge a trust than a will.

REASONS TO SKIP CREATING A TRUST

Remember, estate planning is a process, and your needs may change over time. You don't need to rush into making a trust. Here are a few reasons you might skip one, at least for now.

Cost

As you may have guessed, creating a trust is generally a lot more expensive than drafting a will. Attorney's fees vary based on where you live and the complexity of your situation. While a will costs most people a few hundred dollars, a typical trust costs $1,000–$2,000 or more. If your trust needs third-party administration, that'll add to your expenses.

There may be cheaper DIY options for creating a basic trust. But remember to proceed with caution. Do extensive homework before choosing an online program to build a trust. Research the cost of local attorneys and consider a consultation with one or two before going with a DIY approach.

Money-Saving Tip

Check with your employer to see if you're entitled to free or discounted group legal services as an employee benefit. Employee assistance programs sometimes include estate planning services.

Unless you're in an urgent circumstance where a trust is necessary, you can always decide to create one when it makes more financial sense.

You're Young, Have a Modest Estate, or Own Mostly Non-Probate Assets.

If you're young and healthy or lack valuable assets, you probably don't need a living trust. You may not need any type of trust if you can pass most of your assets to beneficiaries without probate.

If you own a home jointly, rights of survivorship generally allow your surviving spouse to take full ownership. Life insurance policies and retirement accounts have named beneficiaries. And you can make bank accounts and certificates of deposits POD (payable on death). A simple will may be all that's needed to dispose of your car and personal belongings.

Keep in mind, there are situations where it may still make sense to set up a trust even if you're young, have a small financial house, or own assets that could pass to heirs in other ways. You may require a trust if you feel the need to control when and how beneficiaries receive assets.

REVOCABLE AND IRREVOCABLE TRUSTS

Your Goals Determine Their Usage

The definitions of revocable and irrevocable provide a good starting point for understanding the difference between these trusts. But there's a lot more to learn before you make a decision about which one to create. Now's a great time to revisit your estate planning goals to see if establishing a trust helps you fulfill them.

REVOCABLE TRUSTS

The terms revocable trust, revocable living trust, and living trust all describe the same legal arrangement. We call them "living" because you establish and use a revocable trust while you're alive. They're also the most common type of trust used in estate planning.

You can think of a trust as a safe. Since you serve as the trustor and trustee of your living trust, you hold the key to the safe and can add or remove trust property or revoke the trust at any time. You also have the flexibility to amend named replacement trustees or beneficiaries and modify the distribution of the trust's principal.

The assets used to fund your living trust are still considered your property. But trust property, like your bank account or house deed, won't be in your name. After being transferred to the trust (called funding the trust), the owner of the account or house becomes "Your Name, Trustee of the Your Name Living Trust" (or whatever name you give your trust).

You remain in control of your living trust as long as you're alive and competent. Authority to manage your trust shifts to your replacement trustee if you become incapacitated or die. But remember, you have control over your assets even after your death because your trust directs when the trustee can distribute assets to beneficiaries.

One of the main reasons people choose revocable trusts is that assets can pass to beneficiaries after their death without the time and expense of the probate process. By having a trust in place with a named replacement trustee, your loved ones can grieve your passing without worrying about your estate.

While living trusts may help avoid probate, it's essential to understand that your assets won't have protection from creditors or legal action. Since you retain control, a court can force the liquidation of trust property to pay off debts or judgments. The government also considers property in your living trust to be yours, which can impact your ability to qualify for government benefits such as Medicaid.

It's a myth that you get tax benefits from a living trust. If the assets in your trust generate income, you'll be responsible for reporting it when you file your annual return. But including specific language in a trust may help you reduce estate taxes.

A revocable trust becomes irrevocable upon your death. At that point, no one can change the terms of the trust. With the distribution of trust principal to your loved ones, the trust property becomes subject to state and federal estate taxes.

IRREVOCABLE TRUSTS

An irrevocable trust cannot be changed or revoked by you after its creation. You may be allowed to draft an irrevocable trust that reserves some rights, such as amending your trustee or beneficiaries. But changes usually require the approval of a third party.

Think of an irrevocable trust as a locked safe holding property you used to own. Your trustee is the only person with the combination or key. When you transfer assets to the trust, you give up your rights to them. You can't change your mind and remove the property because it's no longer yours.

While it can't be for your benefit, you can request the trustee to access trust assets and provide a benefit for heirs. For instance, you can give a house in the trust to your adult child or pay for a college education. But the trustee uses their discretion to do what's in the best overall interest of the trust.

There are exceptions in some states that allow you to create a trust and receive some benefit from what's in it or retain some control over amending parts of the trust. But these trusts also tend to come with many stipulations.

Most people set up irrevocable trusts to protect assets from lawsuits. If the property in the trust is no longer yours, creditors can't make claims against it. But that protection comes with a price. You'll no longer have the flexibility to move assets around, and you can't benefit from property that's no longer considered yours.

Asset Protection

Doctors, lawyers, accountants, real estate agents, business owners, and other individuals in career fields prone to lawsuits can benefit from using an irrevocable trust as an asset protection strategy.

You can draft irrevocable trusts to achieve different goals. A trust can hold a life insurance policy or be structured for charitable giving. Specific irrevocable trusts are available to support loved ones with special needs. Another type helps a trustor avoid losing their home and life savings if they need long-term care. Keep in mind that trust language and the timing of creating a trust are crucial when it comes to accomplishing your objectives.

While people used to create irrevocable trusts to avoid federal estate taxes, only the very wealthy use them for that purpose now. Unless your estate is worth millions of dollars, federal estate taxes probably won't be an issue.

Providing for children from an earlier marriage is another reason to draft an irrevocable trust. Protecting a surviving spouse or partner is essential when you die. Still, an irrevocable trust can ensure your children receive the assets you planned to pass on to them.

When the distribution of an irrevocable trust's principal to your beneficiaries is complete, the trust ends.

SIMPLE COMPARISON OF REVOCABLE AND IRREVOCABLE TRUSTS	
REVOCABLE TRUST	IRREVOCABLE TRUST
You maintain control	You give up control
Trust assets are still considered yours	Trust assets are no longer yours
Goal is to avoid probate	Goal is asset protection
You get no asset protection	Lacks the flexibility of revocable trusts
You get no estate tax benefits	Provides estate tax benefits for substantial estates

SPECIAL TYPES OF TRUSTS

When Your Needs Are Unique

Revocable living trusts are common because they're flexible and serve the needs of many people. But there are other particular types of trusts you may want to consider as you get further into estate planning.

The decision to create a specific kind of trust should be driven by any unique situations and needs of you and your family. The type and amount of assets you have and the legacy you desire to leave are also factors. Here we introduce you to a few of the more common types of trusts (provisions) people use for asset protection and probate avoidance, and to minimize their estate tax burden.

SPECIAL NEEDS TRUSTS

As its name suggests, you create a special needs trust (SNT) to benefit a person with special needs. But the beneficiary with special needs doesn't own the property placed in the trust. This means their eligibility for needs-based government benefits such as Supplemental Security Income (SSI) or Medicaid isn't affected.

Means Testing

Programs such as SSI and Medicaid are means tested. According to the Social Security Administration, means-tested programs consider "all income and resources that an individual has or can access" and uses them to measure a person's need for assistance.

A revocable or irrevocable "third-party" SNT helps you support a child or relative with special needs. An adult with a disability who has funds or anticipates receiving an inheritance or settlement can also create a self-settled (aka first-party) SNT and be its beneficiary. This type of SNT must be irrevocable.

An SNT is used to cover special and supplemental expenses as outlined by federal law. To prevent the beneficiary from losing government benefits, the trustee administering an SNT must understand what expenses qualify, how to make payments, and any record-keeping requirements.

SPENDTHRIFT TRUST

While it is often called a trust, a spendthrift provision is the language you include in any trust to restrict a beneficiary's use of trust property as collateral for loans or to pay debts. This critical clause is included in most trusts to help prevent access to a beneficiary's trust interests by others, including some creditors.

Including a spendthrift provision in a trust gives you control of the asset distribution to a beneficiary who may be immature, irresponsible with money, or addicted to alcohol, drugs, or gambling.

Your trustee follows your wishes and can help prevent heirs who are "spenders" from blowing their inheritance or having it consumed by legal judgments.

You also don't want the money or property you intended to leave for a loved one to end up in the hands of a criminal. By limiting their access to trust assets, a spendthrift clause acts as a safeguard to prevent vulnerable beneficiaries from becoming fraud victims.

MEDICAID TRUST

As discussed in Chapter 3, it's essential to plan how you'll pay for future long-term care expenses. Purchasing LTC insurance is a choice that may require decades of expensive premium payments before you receive any potential benefit. That's the reason many people consider other options, such as creating a Medicaid trust.

The design of this irrevocable trust is to protect the trust principal from funding nursing home costs. Rather than paying for LTC by spending down your assets to become eligible for Medicaid LTC benefits, you transfer property into a trust at least five years in advance of needing that level of care. When drafted properly and funded early (within the five-year "look back" period), your trust assets generally do not count for Medicaid qualification purposes.

Using this type of trust may help you qualify for Medicaid LTC benefits and leave your beneficiaries with an inheritance. But your choice of nursing home care facilities may be limited. Be sure to consider your needs in addition to those of your loved ones before you decide on creating a Medicaid trust.

More on Medicaid Qualifications

To learn more about Medicaid Long-Term Care Services, visit www .longtermcare.gov. Keep in mind that Medicaid rules and programs vary by state. To learn more about your state's requirements or apply for Medicaid benefits, contact your state medical assistance office.

PET TRUSTS

While you may have friends or family who can take in your animals after you pass away, you can still make sure you're not putting them in a financial burden by caring for your pets.

Creating a pet trust helps ensure someone follows your specific wishes concerning your pet. And it makes funds available to pay for their feeding, grooming, and veterinary care expenses. See Chapter 7, which covers planning for pets in greater detail.

CHARITABLE TRUSTS

Charitable trusts (covered in Chapter 6) are win-win arrangements for those who want planned donations as part of their estate plan. The two main types of charitable trusts are the charitable lead trusts (CLTs) and charitable remainder trusts (CRTs). Both are irrevocable, and the requirements of a CLT and CRT vary. By offering streams of income and tax advantages, they're attractive options for people who prioritize charitable giving as a goal in their overall plan.

AB TRUSTS

An AB trust is a joint trust that separates into two trusts (A and B) when one partner in a married couple dies. You can use this type of trust to accomplish different goals and in unique family situations.

Those with considerable wealth may choose an AB disclaimer trust to avoid federal estate tax liability. But with significant increases to federal estate tax laws and exemptions, AB trusts are not currently necessary for many couples to achieve their objectives.

An AB marital property control trust may also be an option for partners in second marriages. This type of trust allows you to support a surviving spouse while leaving specific assets to children from previous relationships.

AB trusts are involved, however. There may be more straightforward and less expensive options available to meet a couple's estate planning goals.

Other Trusts

There are dozens of other types of trusts and different names for trusts of the same kind. Other examples include annuity trusts, blind trusts, constructive trusts, educational trusts, generation-skipping trusts, land trusts, life insurance trusts, and more. An experienced estate planning attorney can explain the various trust options and help you decide which one you need, if any.

CREATING A LIVING TRUST

Preparation Is Key

Since revocable living trusts are the most commonly used trusts in estate planning, we're going to walk you through the steps of setting one up. We'll cover some steps you can take before talking with an attorney and look at whether DIYing one makes sense. In the following section of this chapter, we'll cover how to fund and manage a living trust.

PREPARING

Thinking back to your goals and reflecting on what you want to accomplish and who you'll include in your trust is an effort well spent. While you'll revisit your trust throughout your lifetime, making mistakes creating it can cost time and money.

Any "homework" you do before starting the process is necessary, no matter if you draft a trust on your own or hire an attorney to assist.

Determine Assets to Fund the Trust

Review the financial inventory you created in Chapter 2 and identify assets that could potentially fund a trust. Examples may include real estate; life insurance; cash, bank, investment or retirement accounts; a small business; collections; and other personal belongings. Make sure to note if they currently have a joint owner or designated beneficiaries.

Identify a Reliable Successor Trustee

You're usually the trustee of your living trust. But you need to consider who can serve as a replacement trustee if you become incapacitated or pass away. You don't want to take this decision lightly, as the trustee role can be a significant responsibility. Since their job is to control and manage your trust, the individual needs to be honest, knowledgeable, and dependable. Also, consider naming an alternate in case the person who agreed can no longer serve. Should you not have a family member or friend to appoint as a replacement trustee, research trust companies in your area to perform the role.

Decide How You Want Trust Assets Managed

During your lifetime, you control the investment and management of the trust principal. You'll also decide how you want assets handled when your replacement trustee takes over. You'll likely base these decisions on the size of your financial house, the types of assets held, the ages and needs of heirs, and how you want assets disbursed. Your trustee's experience with an asset class held in your trust is crucial if they're going to play an ongoing role in its management.

What Is a Trust Company?

Trust companies are corporations that offer trustee services, including trust administration and asset management and protection. They have a fiduciary obligation to take care of trust property and are generally a part of or associated with a traditional lender.

Name Beneficiaries

Your living trust should support you (and a spouse or partner) until your time of death. At that point, your trustee distributes assets to beneficiaries according to the instructions in the trust. Your beneficiaries may be immediate family members, other relatives, friends, or business partners. You can also name a favorite charity as a beneficiary of your living trust.

Determine the Division of Trust Assets Among Beneficiaries

Now that you've determined who gets them, how do you divide trust assets among beneficiaries? The answer to that question depends on who your beneficiaries are and your relationship with them. While there may be hurt feelings if you don't split trust property equally between your children, they may have very different needs. If you plan to disinherit children, make sure to discuss the situation with your attorney.

Decide on the Timing of Asset Distribution

You'll leave instructions to your replacement trustee on when to distribute trust property. In some situations, you'll want beneficiaries to receive what they're due as soon as possible. But suppose you have minor children, loved ones with special needs, or any other circumstance that warrants delaying payments to a beneficiary. In that case, you'll need to state your wishes regarding asset distribution to those individuals clearly.

SEPARATE LIVING TRUSTS OR A JOINT TRUST

If you're married, you need to determine whether you want to create individual trusts or a joint trust. Many couples opt for a joint trust, but individual trusts may be a better option if you need to protect assets from creditors. Separate trusts may also be preferred when either partner expects a large inheritance or if the couple has a prenuptial agreement.

Your attorney can help you determine whether one trust can be structured to achieve your goals or if multiple trusts are needed.

HIRE OR DIY

After completing the preceding steps, it may be evident that your situation is far too complicated to consider using an online document service. While these services continue to grow in popularity, one of the biggest concerns with DIY paperwork is whether it'll be deemed valid in your state. A generic form's ability to meet your unique needs and those of your beneficiaries is another drawback. If you plan to save money by generating trust documents online and reviewing them with a local attorney, check with the attorney first, as they may not be willing to do that.

As explained in Chapter 1, an experienced legal professional is the best option for many people performing estate planning. Your lawyer may be able to suggest alternative options or special provisions for a trust you haven't even considered. Their expertise is also invaluable for the "ins and outs" of trust requirements in your state.

The work doesn't stop with the creation of your trust. In the next section, we cover transferring assets to the trust so it can function as intended. Remember that your property won't avoid probate if your trust doesn't own the investments subject to probating. While you don't need to move all your assets into a trust, failing to fund it correctly is one of the common mistakes people make after setting one up.

FUNDING AND ADMINISTRATION OF A LIVING TRUST

It Won't Work Without Being Funded

Funding a trust you've created is critical if you hope to have it work as designed. Once funded, management of the living trust should include a regular review to note any necessary modifications. These changes could range from simply adding or removing assets to revoking the trust in favor of creating a new one.

FUNDING YOUR TRUST

After creating your trust document, you must fund the trust by transferring assets into it. How you move assets into your trust depends on the type of property you're assigning. If you hold title to an investment, it doesn't become trust property until the title changes from your name to the trustee. Examples of assets you need to retitle include real estate, bank accounts, and brokerage or investment accounts.

When an asset has no legal title, you need to transfer your ownership rights to the trustee by including them on the trust's schedule of assets. Personal property, including jewelry, artwork, clothing, household furnishings, electronics, and vehicles can fall into this category. You'll also need to reassign ownership of some business interests and intellectual property to the trustee if you want them to avoid probate.

You may decide to make your trustee the beneficiary of assets such as your life insurance policy or retirement accounts as well. While these assets do not become trust property, using a trust as a beneficiary allows you to retain control over how and when these assets are distributed to heirs after you pass away.

It takes some effort to complete the paperwork to fund your trust, and it can be a time-consuming process. If you're working with an attorney, they'll usually assist you in transferring real estate into the trust and give you directions on how to add other types of property. But you'll need to make sure the assets become the property of the trust. If, instead, you'd like to do the bulk of the work to save money, ask your attorney which tasks you can do and then have them review all the final transfers.

Pour-Over Wills

If you have a last will and testament, you'll likely need to modify it after creating a trust. By adding a pour-over provision to your will, any assets you don't designate for heirs "pour over" into your trust and get distributed to trust beneficiaries.

The property that transfers to a trust through a pour-over will doesn't avoid probate. However, there may not be much left to pour over if you've moved significant assets to your trust before death. Loved ones may also benefit from smaller estate procedures that speed up the probate process and reduce the costs for any pour-over property not already in your trust.

WHEN TO REVIEW AND AMEND A LIVING TRUST

The flexibility provided by a living trust is one reason people use them in their estate plan. As the trustee, you maintain control and have the ability to add or remove assets at your discretion. You just need to follow the legal procedures to add or remove the property and then update the trust's property schedule: the list of assets a person intends the trust to hold.

After a major life change, you'll also want to consider whether you need to amend your living trust or revise your original plan for distributing your assets.

Your list of beneficiaries, the percent of assets for them to receive, and when they should receive them may look very different a decade or two after creating your trust. You may also need to name an additional replacement trustee or add alternates, requiring you to amend your trust.

You may be able to revise your living trust on your own or work with the online service provider you used to create it. But using an attorney may be a better choice and your preference—depending on the type of change you need to make. If an attorney initially set up your trust, they can advise you on making amendments or revoking it in favor of establishing a new one.

Can a Trust Be Contested?

As is the case with challenging a will, parties with legal standing have grounds to contest a trust under certain circumstances. For example, if a grantor was under duress when creating the trust or the trust has vague language, a probate court may modify or terminate a trust.

SETTLING YOUR LIVING TRUST AFTER YOU DIE

Your living trust becomes irrevocable when you pass away. Your replacement trustee takes over (if they haven't already done so due to your incapacitation) and assumes the responsibility for settling your trust.

Their responsibilities can vary greatly depending on the property in the trust and the instructions you've left to manage and distribute the assets to beneficiaries. To settle a trust, a replacement trustee generally needs to:

1. Communicate with your attorney, the executor of your will, and your heirs and beneficiaries
2. Locate and review essential documents about trust assets
3. Determine the value of trust assets
4. Pay off your remaining debts and file and pay any taxes due
5. Manage trust property and pay ongoing expenses until assets are disbursed to beneficiaries

Since a trustee's responsibilities are significant, they're generally compensated for their efforts from the trust's assets. The IRS considers these payments taxable income, and the trustee must report it on their annual income tax return.

Some states specify how to compensate a trustee, while others allow a trustee to charge a "reasonable" hourly rate. A trustee should keep careful records on trust administration in case anyone challenges their activities or compensation.

TRUSTS AND INCOME TAXES

Who Pays the IRS?

As mentioned earlier, using a revocable living trust does not provide you with any income tax savings. Since, from the IRS's perspective, the assets in a living trust are still your own, you'll continue paying taxes on them as if they were not in a living trust.

When creating other types of trusts, income tax considerations should factor into your decisions. Depending on the assets that make up your trust's principal (i.e., stocks, bonds, real estate), they can generate taxable income in various ways. This includes dividends, royalties, interest, capital gains, business income, and rent. Who pays that income tax depends on who ultimately receives it.

REVOCABLE AND IRREVOCABLE TRUSTS

From an income tax perspective, revocable trusts are the simplest to understand. Any income generated by the revocable trust is taxable to you during your lifetime because you retain control over the principal and terms of a trust.

Revocable trusts are considered "grantor" trusts. In most cases, you report income, deductions, and tax credits for the trust on personal income tax returns. Generally, a separate tax return for the trust won't be required. Instead, you summarize reportable information in a grantor tax information letter. You can file a Form 1041 for informational purposes, but doing so is not required.

In most cases, an irrevocable trust is a separate entity with its own separate tax identification number. It can be either a grantor or non-grantor trust. Federal income taxes apply differently to each type (see following explanation). Income, credits, and deductions for the trust are reported annually for federal income tax purposes using Form 1041.

Grantor Trusts and Federal Taxes

The grantor is the person who contributes funds to a trust, so all tax-related items—income, deductions, and credits—are reported on personal income tax returns. An irrevocable trust can be treated as a grantor trust under certain conditions. An intentionally defective grantor trust (IDGT) might allow you to substitute some of the trust assets with other assets with equal value. Including language like this in your trust document gives you a degree of control, making the income an irrevocable trust earns taxable to you. This means an IDGT is treated as irrevocable for estate taxes but is considered revocable for income tax purposes.

With a grantor trust, you must report the income from the trust on Form 1040 of your individual income tax return.

Non-Grantor Trusts and Federal Taxes

The IRS treats a non-grantor trust as a separate entity responsible for paying income taxes and filing a Form 1041. However, a non-grantor trust is not always responsible for paying taxes on all the income it generates.

When a non-grantor trust distributes a portion of its earned income to a trust beneficiary, it claims a deduction. The trust also issues the beneficiary a Form K-1. It's then the beneficiary's responsibility to pay income tax on the distributions they receive on their income tax return.

Simple or Complex

Non-grantor trusts may be simple or complex. In simple trusts, all the tax year's earnings must be distributed to the beneficiaries. The trustee has the discretion to make distributions as defined in the trust document in a complex trust.

Treatment of Distributions of Interest versus Principal

When it comes to paying taxes on distributions, it makes a difference whether the funds come from the interest earned by assets in the trust or from the trust's principal.

- **Interest.** Once assets become the property of a trust, any interest they accumulate is taxable income. The interest income distributed to a beneficiary is taxable to the person who receives it. A non-grantor trust must pay taxes on the interest income that it does not distribute during the tax year.
- **Principal.** A trust beneficiary does not pay income taxes on distributions they receive from a trust's principal balance. This is because the property was taxed before it was transferred into the trust. If distributions over the amount of the trust's current-year income are made to a beneficiary, the excess payment is assumed to be from the accumulated principal. The excess faces capital gains taxes.
- Any amount distributed to the beneficiary for their benefit is taxable to the beneficiary.
- The trust is responsible for paying income taxes on whatever earnings it retains that were either part of the distributable income or resulted from a change in the trust principal.

TAXATION ON TRUSTS

A trust can face serious taxes on the income it retains. Currently, tax rates on the income it keeps over $100 start at 10 percent and go as high as 37 percent on any income over a mere $12,950. For this reason, most trusts do not want to retain income for long periods. Undistributed investment income held by trusts may also be subjected to an additional tax called the net investment income tax, or NIIT.

Trust income could be taxed at the state level too. Some trusts may owe no state taxes, while others may owe tax in more than one state. This depends on the type of trust and income, along with the residential locations of the grantor, trustee, and beneficiary. You'll need to speak with an attorney or tax professional to learn more about specific types of trusts and how their taxation works in your state.

Reducing Estate Taxes with Trusts

You know a living trust won't save you any income taxes, and the use of a living trust alone does not reduce estate taxes. But those with substantial assets may wish to combine a living trust with other types of trusts to provide some estate tax savings or postpone the tax. These types of trusts include:

- AB disclaimer trusts
- Charitable trusts
- Generation-skipping trusts
- Grantor-retained interest trusts
- Irrevocable life insurance trusts
- Qualified terminable interest property trusts (QTIPs)

An experienced estate planning attorney can help you decide if any of these types of trusts are right for you.

Chapter 6

Estates and Taxation

Death and taxes. While neither is a fun topic, both are sure things, as the saying goes. Although avoiding them altogether is out of the question, there are actions you can take to try to postpone their happening or lessen their impact. As your wealth increases and your financial house becomes more intricate, the tax code can go from being a bit confusing to downright baffling at times. But with information comes knowledge and understanding.

The process of tax planning can help you identify ways to lower the amount of taxes you owe legally. Through it, think both broadly—your lifetime tax burden—and more narrowly to reduce your taxes in a given year.

INCOME TAXES AND TAX PLANNING BASICS

Adulting with the IRS

You might only think about the taxes you pay when looking at pay-stubs, sending in your annual property taxes, or preparing year-end income tax returns. But spending time on annual tax planning can save you money. A little effort can keep you from overpaying your tax obligations now and for years to come. It can also help you leave more to heirs and beneficiaries and help them keep more of your gift.

There are several ways to approach yearly tax planning, but there are mainly three basic techniques: controlling adjusted gross income, increasing tax deductions, and using qualifying tax credits. As you consider each of these tax-saving strategies, you'll see how saving money for the future can also reward you now.

UNDERSTANDING TAXES

US federal income taxes are progressive taxes. Progressive tax systems take a larger percentage of income from those with higher earnings than those with lower wages. This is because those with more significant income and assets are considered to have the ability to pay increasing amounts of tax. Current tax rates range from 10 percent for the lowest earners to 37 percent for those with the highest income. An explanation of how this works and a chart of income tax brackets are in this chapter's next section.

Taxable Income

Growing your income is typically considered a good thing. One potential downside of receiving more income is an increasing tax liability. And no matter how you feel about taxes, you probably aren't interested in paying more than you should.

The First Federal Income Tax

On February 25, 1913, federal income tax became law through the Sixteenth Amendment of the US Constitution. It gave Congress the ability to tax individual and business income. The first Form 1040 tax return was issued in January 1914 with one page of instructions; today, it includes more than one hundred pages of instructions.

When determining taxes owed, we start with our annual gross income—all income earned and received as money, property, or services within a given year. Examples of income are wages, tips, bonuses, interest, dividends, cash payments, rents received, and business earnings.

We then subtract any adjustments we qualify for, such as student loan interest and health savings account or traditional IRA contributions, to arrive at our adjusted gross income (AGI). These qualifying adjustments are commonly referred to as above-the-line tax deductions because they occur above the AGI. Next, we determine below-the-line deductions.

Standard versus Itemized

The standard deduction is an amount all taxpayers can take to lower their taxable income. The IRS established the standard deduction to ensure all taxpayers can exclude some income from federal income tax. The amount varies depending on filing status—single, joint, or head of household—and is set each year by Congress. For many of us, the standard deduction will apply. For some, itemizing can make more sense.

When your allowable itemized deductions—i.e., property taxes, mortgage interest, uncovered medical or dental expenses, charitable contributions—total more than the standard deduction amount, you might lower your tax bill by claiming these itemized deductions. You'll need to run some calculations to be sure.

Subtracting either the standard or the allowable itemized deductions from your AGI brings you to your taxable income amount. From there, you determine your tax according to the current year tax instructions, add or subtract any additional qualifying tax or tax credits, and arrive at your total tax due.

Deductions versus Credits

- **Tax Adjustments:** Specific expenses, payments, contributions, and fees you can subtract from total income.
- **Tax Deductions:** Allowable personal (or business) expenses that reduce the income subject to tax.
- **Tax Credits:** An allowable reduction in the amount of tax owed to the Internal Revenue Service (IRS).

To determine if you owe the IRS (or if you're due a refund), subtract tax payments you've made throughout the year and additional eligible tax credits from your total tax.

CONTROLLING TAXES

Congress establishes the tax code, including the annual standard deduction, along with tax credits and adjustments. With tax credits and certain adjustments, you either qualify for them, or you don't. The important thing is paying attention to them and using them to your advantage when they do apply.

For example, you might be paying college tuition this year. In that case, you could be eligible for the American Opportunity Tax Credit or the Lifetime Learning Credit. These tax credits can help you save $2,000 or more per year when you're eligible for them. Remember, you deduct tax credits from your total tax, so a $2,000 tax credit keeps $2,000 in your pocket.

On the other hand, tax adjustments and deductions reduce the amount of your income that's taxed. So, the adjustment or deduction you're eligible for doesn't save you dollar-for-dollar, but rather saves you the percentage of your tax rate. For example, if you take a standard tax deduction of $12,550 and you're in the 22 percent tax bracket, you could save up to $2,761 in taxes ($12,550 × 22 percent = $2,761) depending on your total taxable income.

By using tax planning strategies to postpone, shift, or change income and expenses, you could optimize tax adjustments, deductions, and credits to reduce your annual tax bill. We'll discuss some short- and long-term strategies in the rest of this chapter to help minimize taxes throughout your lifetime and for those who later inherit your assets.

BUILDING TAX-ADVANTAGED WEALTH

Keeping More Money in Your Estate

Tax contributions are essential for society and not something we can avoid. But overpaying them isn't good for your wallet. Understanding how earning money and accumulating wealth affect future tax liabilities is something everyone can benefit from, no matter your income or net worth. Tax planning strategies to save money might include deferring income, shifting expenses, or holding on to assets for specific periods to change how they're taxed.

TAX AWARENESS

Being aware of the tax implications of different income sources, how and when you pay for certain expenses, and where and how you invest can affect what you owe now and in the future. With a better awareness of the tax code and available incentives for saving and investing, you can minimize the taxes you pay and maximize estate growth.

Types of Income and Tax Rates

Here's a quick review of the main types of income and how the earnings from each affect your tax bill.

Earned Income

Earned, or active, income is what you're probably most familiar with. Also called ordinary income, this is dispersed in wages, salaries, commissions, bonuses, and tips. Unemployment compensation and freelance or business income are other forms of earned income. Additionally, this category includes money received from pensions, 401(k) and traditional IRA distributions, rental income, interest received from bank accounts, CDs, most bonds, and personal loans made to others.

Earned income is taxed at marginal tax rates, as shown in the IRS tax brackets. The amount of your income that falls within the brackets is taxed at the corresponding tax rate.

2021 FEDERAL INCOME TAX BRACKETS AND RATES FOR SINGLE FILERS, MARRIED COUPLES FILING JOINTLY, AND HEADS OF HOUSEHOLDS			
RATE	FOR UNMARRIED INDIVIDUALS	FOR MARRIED INDIVIDUALS FILING JOINT RETURNS	FOR HEADS OF HOUSEHOLDS
10 percent	Up to $9,950	Up to $19,900	Up to $14,200
12 percent	$9,951 to $40,525	$19,901 to $81,050	$14,201 to $54,200
22 percent	$40,526 to $86,375	$81,051 to $172,750	$54,201 to $86,350
24 percent	$86,376 to $164,925	$172,751 to $329,850	$86,351 to $164,900
32 percent	$164,926 to $209,425	$329,851 to $418,850	$164,901 to $209,400
35 percent	$209,426 to $523,600	$418,850 to $628,300	$209,401 to $523,600
37 percent	Over $523,600	Over $628,300	Over $523,600
Source: Internal Revenue Service			

Example

If you're single and have $52,345 in taxable income, you'll pay:

- 10 percent on the first $9,950 = $995
- 12 percent on earnings from $9,951 to $40,525 or $30,574 = $3,669
- 22 percent on earnings from $40,525 to $52,345 or $11,820 = $2,600
- Total tax = $7,264 ($995 + $3,669 + $2,600)

Investment Income

Investment or portfolio income is earned from various investing activities and is primarily received as capital gains and dividends.

Capital gains income is essentially the profit you make when selling an investment (stocks or real estate) for more than you paid. If you owned the investment for less than twelve months, the profit is considered a short-term gain. For assets held more than one year, it's deemed a long-term gain.

Short-term capital gains are taxed as ordinary income, similar to interest payments. Long-term capital gains incur tax according to the capital gains tax brackets, currently 0 percent, 15 percent, and 20 percent.

2021 LONG-TERM CAPITAL GAINS TAX RATES			
RATE	UNMARRIED	MARRIED FILING JOINTLY	HEAD OF HOUSEHOLD
0 percent	Up to $40,400	Up to $80,800	Up to $54,100
15 percent	$40,401 to $445,850	$80,801 to $501,600	$54,101 to $473,750
20 percent	Over $445,851	Over $501,601	Over $473,751
Source: Internal Revenue Service			

Most dividend income (paid on stocks) is taxed at long-term capital gains rates, but there could be exceptions that cause them to be taxed at ordinary income rates.

TAX-ADVANTAGED STRATEGIES TO INCREASE WEALTH

We can use some tax planning strategies to shift or change income or expenses annually to not overpay taxes. When we combine those strategies with tax-advantaged accounts to save and invest, we also efficiently build wealth for the future.

Shifting or Changing Taxable Income

Shifting income, bunching deductions, or timing the sale of investments from one year to another may keep your income within a lower bracket and tax rate.

For example, income such as bonuses, dividends, or year-end payments and deductible expenses such as charitable donations, medical costs, or property taxes might be shifted from year to year to pay less tax in a given year.

Likewise, holding a stock for more than one year before selling it at a profit changes the tax from short-term capital gains to long-term capital gains rates. Remember, the sale of an asset held less than 365 days causes the profit on that sale to be taxed as ordinary income.

Using either of these tax savings strategies will require some planning and good record-keeping but can be well worth your time.

Using Tax-Advantaged Accounts

You won't (and shouldn't) base all your financial decisions on the tax code. But you'll find it beneficial to use tax-advantaged accounts in your wealth-building plans as often as you can.

For Retirement

By making contributions to tax-deferred accounts such as traditional 401(k)s and IRAs, you can delay paying income tax on those funds until a later date. This is most beneficial if your income puts you in a high-income tax bracket now, and you expect to be in a lower tax bracket when withdrawing the money in retirement. On the other hand, if you're in a low-income bracket today, you may choose to use Roth accounts to pay a lower tax rate now and benefit from tax-free withdrawals in the future. Inherited Roth funds are also tax-free to beneficiaries.

Since we can't predict future tax brackets and rates, utilizing both types of tax-advantaged accounts is a strategy worth considering.

For Education Expenses

You can save for a child's or grandchild's education in a tax-advantaged way through savings plans such as popular 529 Plans. Contributions are made after tax, but they grow tax deferred. When savings withdrawals pay for qualified education expenses, they're tax-free.

For Dependent Care Expenses

A Dependent Care Flexible Savings Account (DCFSA) is an employer-sponsored benefit that allows you to stash tax-deferred funds away to pay for eligible expenses. These include typical daycare costs (including some adult daycare), nanny expenses, preschool, after-school care, and seasonal day camps. DCFSAs have contribution limits and face a "use-it-or-lose-it" rule, so you must carefully estimate annual out-of-pocket expenses before committing contributions to them.

For Medical Expenses

Similar to a Dependent Care FSA is the Health FSA. You can save money when you use pre-tax contributions to pay for various healthcare expenses. This can include office visit copays, insurance deductibles, prescriptions, dental and vision care, and medical supplies for you and eligible dependents. But these FSA funds are also subject to the "use-it-or-lose-it" rule, so you need to plan accordingly.

Health savings accounts (HSAs) are another type of account used to pay for healthcare expenses. However, HSAs are restricted to those with a high-deductible health insurance plan (HDHP). Unlike a Health FSA, you won't lose the money in an HSA if you don't use it. Instead, it can continue to grow tax deferred. They do have annual contribution limits, but nontaxed contributions grow tax deferred. When used on qualifying medical expenses, those funds are tax-free. Money withdrawn before age sixty-five for nonqualifying medical expenses is subject to income tax and a 20 percent penalty. Any money remaining once you turn sixty-five can be used for non-healthcare costs, making it more attractive because it increases its usefulness in retirement.

Utilizing tax-advantaged accounts and maxing them out when possible can keep more money in your estate. Whether you invest pre- or post-tax will be dependent on earnings, financial goals, and when you feel it's best to pay the income tax. It may be tempting to pay the tax later. Yet paying now and receiving tax-free withdrawals in the future is something you'll want to consider seriously.

ESTATE AND INHERITANCE TAXES

When You Have Millions

You understand you pay taxes during your lifetime. But the bad news is your estate might pay taxes when you die. Some of your heirs could also be required to pay tax on the inheritance you leave them.

The good news? Estate and inheritance taxes will likely not apply to you or your heirs. But if they do, there are ways to limit them.

With that said, everyone needs to understand how these tax laws work because Congress can change them, and you could inherit substantial wealth from others. While it might be difficult to imagine a tax burden today, you could potentially face one in the future.

FEDERAL ESTATE TAXES

For the privilege of transferring property upon your death, the IRS may charge your estate with an estate tax. The fair market value (FMV) of everything you own or have interests in at your time of death factors into whether your estate pays the tax.

Your "gross estate" is the total FMV of all assets—cash, securities, real estate, insurance, trusts, annuities, business interests, and other investments—not their initial value at the time of purchase or receipt.

From your gross estate, some allowed deductions are subtracted to calculate your "taxable estate." Allowable deductions include mortgages, other debts, property passing to a surviving spouse, assets donated to qualified charities, funeral expenses, estate administration expenses, and losses suffered by the estate during its management after your death. Once your taxable estate is determined, the value of any lifetime taxable gifts (discussed later) is added to it to determine if estate taxes apply.

Although all US citizens' estates are subject to the federal estate tax, most will never pay it because of a generous estate tax exemption ($11.7 million per individual in 2021). Only estates exceeding the exemption after combining their taxable estate value with the total value of prior taxable gifts will need to file a federal estate tax return (Form 706).

Should the amount of your estate exceed the estate tax exemption, it could pay a sizable amount of taxes. Current estate tax rates range from 18 percent to 39 percent on taxable amounts of $1 to $1 million, over the allowable exclusion. And a whopping 40 percent on all taxable parts over $1 million.

Generation-Skipping Transfers (GST) and Taxes

Decades ago, wealthy individuals could eliminate taxes on a substantial amount of their wealth by transferring it to grandchildren instead of their children.

A simple example is if someone had $15 million, they might transfer $10 million to their grandchildren while they were alive, leaving $5 million in their estate for their children to inherit upon their death. By doing this, they could preserve wealth for the younger generations because $10 million escaped estate taxes (up to 60 percent). If they left the whole $15 million to their children instead, it would be taxed at their time of death and then again at their children's time of death. This would ultimately leave less money for the grandchildren.

Congress first tried to reduce this practice in 1976 and later passed the Tax Reform Act of 1986 to tax these generation-skipping wealth transfers. Fortunately (or unfortunately), most of us will never have to worry about paying the generation-skipping transfer tax (GSTT) either. For those concerned about the GSTT, speak with an estate planning attorney to understand specifics about exemptions, exclusions, and how a trust may benefit you.

While many estates will not require a federal estate tax return or payment of the GSTT, some may face a state estate tax.

STATE ESTATE TAXES

A dozen states and the District of Columbia currently enforce an estate tax. While they all now have lower estate tax exemptions than the federal government, that may not always be the case.

The following states currently tax the estates of deceased residents with rates ranging from 0.8–20 percent.

- Connecticut
- District of Columbia
- Hawaii
- Illinois
- Maine
- Maryland
- Massachusetts
- Minnesota
- New York
- Oregon
- Rhode Island
- Vermont
- Washington

Inheritance Taxes

The federal government does not impose any inheritance taxes, but a handful of states do. The inheritance tax is paid by the heirs rather than the estate itself. Currently, heirs of deceased residents from Iowa, Kentucky, Maryland, Nebraska, New Jersey, and Pennsylvania may face an inheritance tax.

Surviving spouses are typically exempt from state inheritance tax, but some states may tax surviving children at a low rate. Usually, other relatives or friends who are named beneficiaries face higher inheritance tax rates. So, if you live in Pennsylvania and your rich great-aunt leaves you a few million dollars, don't go buying a Ferrari and a mansion without first knowing how much you'll owe the state.

Tax on Assets You Receive Through Inheritance

Most assets, including cash, bank accounts, life insurance proceeds, CDs, stocks and bonds, real estate, cars, personal items, and Roth IRAs, are usually not taxable at inheritance. Some transactions, such as withdrawals from a traditional IRA or capital gains on an asset's sale, are taxable and reported as income.

LIMITING ESTATE TAXES

If you're fortunate enough to build a substantial financial house, you might use the following strategies during your lifetime to reduce the taxes your estate or heirs pay later.

1. **Enjoy:** Spend assets for your pleasure instead of leaving them behind for others.
2. **Gift:** Share some assets with loved ones while you can see them enjoyed (discussed in the next section).
3. **Donate:** Give part of your assets to a qualifying charity or establish a donor-advised fund (explained later in the chapter).

4. **Shield:** Create a trust to legally shelter some assets from taxes (mentioned later in the chapter and covered in Chapter 5).
5. **Relocate:** While it may seem like a drastic choice, some people choose to move so they are no longer a resident of a state with an estate or inheritance tax.

Another option to consider is transforming some assets, such as converting traditional retirement accounts to Roth IRAs. Since income tax must be paid on withdrawals or distributions from all traditional (pre-tax) retirement accounts, beneficiaries of those accounts eventually face paying taxes on them. However, you could transform some of those pre-tax funds into after-tax funds by paying the income tax during a Roth conversion. Your heirs will then enjoy tax-free distributions from the inherited Roth account. This process can be a bit complicated, so it's best to consult a tax or financial professional before executing the strategy to avoid costly mistakes.

GIFTS AND TAXES

Sharing with Others (Limiting Uncle Sam's Reach)

When all your financial needs are met, with no fear of running out of money before death, you might consider gifting cash or other assets to heirs during your lifetime, instead of later in a will or trust. This allows you to witness how the gifts help or bring joy to others. But gifting someone substantial amounts of money or property during your lifetime can subject you to the federal gift tax.

In this section, we'll explore ways to avoid gift taxes or at least reduce them as much as possible. While gifting should not be dependent on tax savings, it could be a nice bonus depending on your estate's size.

WHAT'S A GIFT?

First, let's look at what a gift is from a legal perspective.

A voluntary and permanent transfer of money or property to another individual or organization without receiving something of equal value in return is considered a gift. In the IRS's eyes, vital elements of a legal gift transaction are that it be unforced for both parties, not temporary, and be a complete transfer of control over the asset.

In other words, someone cannot force you into giving a gift. You cannot pressure someone into taking a gift. And you cannot receive any future benefits from the asset you give away.

Examples of legal gifts you might give someone include:

- Handing them cash or an item of value
- Retitling real estate or a motor vehicle in their name
- Transferring ownership of stocks or bonds to them
- Selling something to them at less than its full market value
- Providing them with an interest-free or very-low-interest loan or forgiving a debt they owe you

THE FEDERAL GIFT TAX

When giving someone (other than your spouse) assets during a calendar year with a total value over a certain amount, you may face a gift tax. This amount is called an annual exclusion and is determined by federal law. Any gift with a value under the annual exclusion will not be taxed. For tax purposes, you calculate the value of a gift that isn't cash by taking the FMV of the gift on the date it was given and subtracting any outstanding debts. As the giver of the asset, you're responsible for any gift tax, not the recipient.

Since you can use the federal gift tax exclusion every year, a sizable piece of your estate can be given away when you use it multiple times.

The Annual Exclusion

The annual exclusion amount for gifts is currently $15,000 per receiver. If you're married and your spouse agrees to gift as well, you can give up to $30,000 per year, per individual recipient. This means you can give $15,000 annually to any number of people without facing a gift tax. Give one person $15,000 or give five different people $15,000 each in a calendar year, and you won't trigger any gift taxes.

Any gift value over the annual exclusion amount could result in gift taxes. If you give $25,000 to a sister, $10,000 could be subject to the gift tax. However, unless the taxable amount of your total life-time gifts exceeds the federal estate tax exemption (currently $11.7 million), you may not ever pay the tax. You may pay a state estate tax depending on its exemption amount.

So, in addition to being aware of the annual amount of gifting you can do without facing federal gift tax (currently $15,000), you need to keep in mind the federal estate tax exemption discussed in the previous section. Also, be aware some states have a gift tax as well with different exemption amounts.

When making gifts over the amount of your annual exclusion in a given year, you must report them to the IRS when filing your regular income tax return (on Form 709). This is a requirement, even though you may not have to pay the gift tax.

Gift Tax Exemptions

When the total of all taxable gifts you hand out to others before your death is below the federal estate tax exemption, no gift taxes are owed. But this does reduce the amount of your federal estate tax exemption used to determine if your estate will owe taxes after you die. Again, this is likely not to apply to most of us since the current exemption amount is $11.7 million. But it's something to be aware of since that amount is scheduled to reduce to $5 million (indexed to inflation) in 2026. Congress can also change the tax code and further lower (or increase) the exemption amount in future years.

Let's look at a simplified example. Suppose you gave away $700,000 in taxable gifts this year. Your estate tax exemption would decrease by that amount to become $11 million. If you then die with a taxable estate of $8 million, your estate would not face federal estate taxes. However, if your taxable estate's value is $12 million, it would face estate tax on the $1 million excess.

Inflation and Taxes

Using the United States Chained Consumer Price Index (CPI)—the measurement of price levels on consumer goods and services over time—the IRS annually factors inflation into tax rates. Contribution limits, exclusions, exemptions, and other amounts are also indexed to help protect taxpayers from losing benefits and financial values.

Additional Gift Exemptions

Assets of any value given to a tax-exempt charitable organization or political organization are free from federal gift tax. You can also avoid gift taxes on money given and used to pay for someone's education or medical expenses. The essential condition here is that the money must be paid directly to the educational institution or medical provider and not to the person who benefits. If you give $25,000 directly to your son to pay a hospital bill, it would be considered a gift and trigger the gift tax.

To Gift or Not to Gift

We've only provided the "tip of the iceberg" on the federal gift tax and how the annual exclusion might be used to give generously and potentially save on taxes. There's much more to know about when you'd file a gift tax return and pay any taxes due, who you can give property to, and what you can or can't give. Plus, there are special rules in the tax code you'll need to follow when giving certain property types or when gifting to minors.

Be sure to conduct further research to be aware of all the benefits and drawbacks of gifting and consider speaking with and using financial and legal professionals to avoid potential mistakes.

CHARITABLE REMAINDER TRUSTS AND DONOR-ADVISED FUNDS

Maximizing Your Donations

Many of us are privileged enough to be able to donate to charities. Typically, to obtain an income tax deduction for charitable contributions, you must itemize deductions on your annual tax return. But some years, you might not have total itemized deductions that exceed the standard deduction amount. In that case, you could consider lumping donations into a single tax year to maximize tax savings. For example, you may choose to donate in one year the gifts you might otherwise spread out over two or three years and then skip giving in the other years.

Additional tax-efficient gifting methods include using either a charitable trust or a donor-advised fund (or both).

DONOR-ADVISED FUNDS

A donor-advised fund (DAF) is a charitable giving account you (the donor) establish with a qualified nonprofit (the sponsoring organization) in exchange for immediate tax deductions. The account is funded by irrevocable contributions—meaning you can't take them back—and is administered and managed by the sponsoring organization. The organization has legal control over all funds you contribute. Still, you advise them on investing and distributing the money in the account over time.

This means you can give a sponsoring organization $30,000 in a calendar year and take a tax write-off the same year. Then, you can make requests for the money to be sent to charities in later years. These requests are known as recommending a grant. The contributed money grows tax-free until donated to the charities.

You can make a one-time contribution to a DAF or ongoing contributions. However, most sponsoring organizations have a minimum dollar requirement to open an account. Some have minimums for additional contributions made in later years. All typically have a minimum dollar grant request requirement and may limit the number of requests you can make per year.

Benefits of DAFs

The primary benefit of DAFs is the ability to receive a tax deduction the year you contribute money. This makes DAFs helpful for any high-income earning years when you want to minimize taxes but spread the actual giving to charities over time.

Additional benefits include:

- Less record-keeping for you since the sponsoring organization administers the fund
- Ability to make donations anonymously or "in memoriam"
- Potential to donate assets other than money to a charity

Some sponsoring organizations will accept stocks, real estate, part of a business, or alternative assets like art. They can then convert them to cash for donation to charities you name.

Downsides of DAFs

A couple of previously mentioned drawbacks to DAFs are that once you contribute money, it's no longer yours, and there are minimum dollar requirements for funding. Additional downsides can include limited investment options within a fund and fees charged by the sponsoring organization. There may also be restrictions on where and how money is distributed and if the DAF can be passed on to heirs.

CHARITABLE TRUSTS

As briefly mentioned in Chapter 5, there are two main types of charitable trusts: the charitable remainder trust (CRT) and the charitable lead trust (CLT). Both share some benefits with DAFs but have some significant differences too. These include the timing of tax deductions, the amount of time the trust can exist, and who ultimately receives the income and assets from the trust at the end of its term.

As with DAFs, contributions to either a CRT or CLT are irrevocable. Once you give property to the trust, you can't take it back. Also like DAFs, donations from the trust must be made to nonprofits with tax-exempt status under Section 501(c)(3) of the Internal Revenue Code.

Unlike DAFs, charitable trusts are limited in duration (twenty years or less). You must determine the recipient charity upfront. And your income tax break doesn't necessarily come in the year you donate funds. Next, we take a look at the difference between the CRT and CLT.

Charitable Remainder Trusts (CRTs)

A CRT is a trust you establish with assets to benefit an income beneficiary (you or someone else) and a final beneficiary (the charity). A CRT can exist for up to twenty years but stops upon your death. At that time, assets pass on to the charity. The income beneficiary receives a specific dollar amount or percentage of the trust's value, i.e., $10,000 or 10 percent per year, for a predetermined amount of time or until their death or yours.

If the income beneficiary is anyone other than you or your spouse, payments made to them are considered a taxable gift. Annual payments exceeding the IRS gift tax exemption face the gift tax on the overage. You must file an appropriate gift tax return in that case. When a CRT ends and the trust's principal transfers to the charity, it's no longer part of your taxable estate and no longer subject to gift or estate taxes.

The amount and timing of income tax deductions depend on various factors. These include when the property was gifted to the charity, the life expectancy of the income beneficiary, current interest rates, and the estimated value of the trust assets when they'll pass to the charity.

Charitable Lead Trusts (CLTs)

A charitable lead trust (CLT) is the opposite of a CRT. The charity is the income beneficiary, and you or someone you choose is the final beneficiary of a CLT. There's typically no income tax advantage with a CLT. Still, it does provide a way for the wealthy to make tax-free gifts to family members while also benefiting a charity for several years.

Gifting Appreciated Assets

One factor making a DAF, CRT, or CLT especially attractive is the ability to donate highly appreciated property to them without paying any capital gains tax on the assets upfront, if at all.

Maximizing Tax-Advantaged Gifting

To provide maximum tax benefits and flexible gifting, some people utilize both a DAF and a CRT together by naming the DAF as the CRT's final beneficiary.

Chapter 7

Situations Requiring Careful Consideration

We've covered a lot up to this point. But there are several situations that could use further attention. Single people, those with a blended family, or individuals considering disinheriting someone should read this chapter. Those with pets, a small business, or a loved one with a disability should read too. And so should everyone else. Because life's uncertain, and you could find yourself in one of those situations someday.

ESTATE PLANNING FOR BLENDED FAMILIES

Protecting Yours, Mine, and Ours

Estate plans share many of the same characteristics, but you need to design a plan to meet your family's unique needs. While it's vital for everyone, estate planning takes on more significance when you have a blended family. Planning for the worst may seem like you're taking a negative view of your family. But hoping for the best isn't a smart estate planning move whether you have a traditional family unit or not. While you may be one big happy clan today, don't mistakenly assume there won't be a serious conflict between family members in the future.

If you fail to plan, some heirs may not end up receiving your assets. Sadly, this may damage relationships in your family beyond repair. A blended household needs an estate plan with specific provisions to protect everyone, no matter which spouse passes away first.

BLENDED FAMILIES AND WHAT CAN GO WRONG

Many consider a blended family to be a couple with children they have from previous relationships along with any children they've had together. But blended families take many forms. Anyone with a step, half, or "bonus" parent, sibling, or child is part of a blended family.

The age span of blended family members can also vary greatly. A second or subsequent marriage can happen in your twenties or many decades later. In blended families, beneficiaries can range from minor children to adults who have a blended family of their own. This helps explain why a blended family's estate planning can be more complicated.

Here are two examples of what can go wrong for a blended family:

Situation #1

A big mistake couples make after blending their busy lives is failing to draft a new will or other essential estate planning documents. If one partner were to die without a will, they would be intestate, and their estate would be subject to probate.

Assets are deemed community or separate property depending on how and when they're acquired and the state's laws where owners hold property. Intestate succession laws determine which property (and in what percentage) goes to a surviving spouse or dependents of the deceased.

If you haven't added a new spouse to your home's title, your children or a family member may take ownership instead. An inheritance you received and planned to give to your kids may be commingled with funds in a joint bank account that passes to your spouse.

While family members may do what's "right" and follow your wishes, they may not even know what plans you had for those assets.

Situation #2

Some couples do draft wills and other essential documents after blending their families. But children of the first spouse to die may end up disinherited if a couple uses a will-based plan.

Many couples choose to leave their entire estate to their surviving spouse. A surviving spouse may change their will, get remarried, or make other moves with all their assets. When the second spouse passes away, their estate goes to their new spouse or biological children, disinheriting the first spouse's children altogether.

There are plenty of other issues that can arise with estates and blended families. An ex-spouse may end up with an asset because beneficiary designations weren't updated on accounts and policies. Children of a deceased spouse may also sue a spendthrift stepparent if they fear a threat to their future inheritance.

ESTATE PLANNING STRATEGIES FOR BLENDED FAMILIES

A couple with a blended family needs to have clear and open communication about their assets, who they belong to, and their estate planning goals. While these may be challenging and emotional conversations, they're essential to determine who needs to be provided for and to what degree. Then an estate plan can be structured around those decisions.

Due to the complexity of situations in many blended families, this isn't something you should DIY. A financial advisor and experienced estate planning attorney can prove invaluable to ensure your family and assets have protection in these situations.

Here are a few examples of estate planning strategies for blended families.

Give Gifts While You're Alive

One way to make sure children receive part of your estate is to give them assets while you're alive. You won't have to depend on your spouse or an executor or trustee if you control the funds or property. Remember, large gifts may be subject to the federal gift tax (Chapter 6).

Immediate Inheritances to Children

It can cause hard feelings between family members when an estate plan provides for your spouse but requires your children to wait for their expected inheritance. One way to address this situation is to leave an immediate gift of money or personal property to your children at your time of death. While you can make provisions that they'll receive assets outright, you can also hold a balance for children in a trust. A life insurance policy is another way to provide an inheritance to your children. However, minors won't have immediate access to it.

Prenups or Postnups

These legal contracts establish the property rights and financial responsibilities of each spouse during the marriage. They may also specify how to distribute current and future assets upon one spouse's death, protecting the children in a blended family.

Establishment of a Trust

By creating a trust, you can provide for your spouse at the time of your death while ensuring assets pass to your children in the end. Some of these trusts include marital trusts, family trusts, AB or ABC trusts, and qualified terminable interest property trusts (QTIPs).

As discussed in Chapter 5, you can use various trust structures to meet your specific goals. An experienced attorney can help you choose which type of trust can help accomplish your goals and address your blended family's needs.

PLANNING YOUR ESTATE AS AN UNMARRIED COUPLE

When Failing to Plan Is Really Planning to Fail

Unmarried couples come in many forms. It can be two people in a relationship who cohabitate and have children together, life partners who have no children and live in separate homes, and plenty of arrangements in between.

While there are many ways to be an unmarried couple, what isn't unique are the problems that can occur when one partner in these relationships becomes incapacitated or passes away. An unmarried couple who procrastinates on creating necessary estate planning paperwork can put their significant other into challenging situations.

ESTATE PLANNING IS ESSENTIAL FOR UNMARRIED COUPLES

It might surprise you to learn that when one partner dies, the surviving partner in an unmarried couple could face eviction from a home they shared, or be left with nothing from their estate. Partners can mistakenly exclude significant others from making urgent medical decisions or managing their finances at a critical time. That's why it's necessary for committed couples who aren't married to take estate planning seriously.

Mistakes unmarried couples make include failing to understand state laws about inheritance rights or intestate succession, and assuming their family will always "do the right thing" and include their partner when something terrible happens.

But you can take steps today to begin an estate plan that protects you both and any children who are part of your relationship.

Titling Accounts and Property

If your goal is to provide for another, one of the first things you can do as an unmarried couple is to look at how assets are titled and avoid probate. This includes real estate, cars, bank accounts, stocks and bonds, business interests, and more.

You need to decide whether you want the joint property to go to your significant other or be split between them and your heirs when you die. This determines whether you want to own the property as tenants in common or as joint tenants with rights of survivorship. You can read more about these options in Chapter 2.

Another way to avoid probate and make sure others follow your wishes is to have property owned by a revocable living trust. A trust can be structured to accomplish your goals, and since it's revocable, there is always the option to change it over time.

You can also designate your significant other as the beneficiary of bank or brokerage accounts and life insurance policies. This allows the asset to bypass probate and go directly to your partner.

What about a Domestic Partnership?

A domestic partnership is an alternative to marriage, giving couples some legal benefits. The requirements and advantages of domestic legal partnerships vary by state. Make sure to research this option before assuming it's the right move for you and your partner.

Wills and Trusts

The key documents in an estate plan that determine how assets will get passed to heirs and beneficiaries are a will and a trust.

A will allows you to leave individually owned property to whoever you'd like. These include all your assets without a beneficiary or POD/TOD designations and those not jointly owned or held in trust. This property will still go through probate, but you can name your significant other as a beneficiary in your will. (Note: You may have to leave your house to your minor children if you live in a state with specific Homestead Protection laws.)

A living trust is another option that allows you (as trustee) to control the property your trust holds while also being the beneficiary of it while you're alive. You can name your significant other as a beneficiary of some (or all) of the property in the trust, so it passes directly to them when you die.

Trusts allow you to avoid probate, maintain privacy, and determine when and how much of your estate to distribute to beneficiaries. In the event of incapacitation, your successor trustee can also take over and manage your finances.

Without having a will or trust in place, intestate succession laws will likely prevent your partner from receiving assets you wanted them to have. Instead, children, grandchildren, parents, siblings, and other relatives will be in line to receive your property.

Other Estate Planning Documents

Both unmarried partners should also consider signing a HIPAA authorization and creating an advance directive and durable power of attorney.

These forms can allow your partner access to healthcare information and give them legal authority to make medical decisions for you if you're unable. You can also designate your significant other as the person in charge of managing your finances if you're incapacitated.

But you need to understand this paperwork and the information and powers you're assigning to your partner. While they help express your intentions and prevent a situation like conservatorship, you don't have to name a partner as your agent on these forms if you have reservations.

More for Unmarried Couples to Consider

You can do other things to help protect both of you—financially and emotionally—if you become incapacitated or pass away.

1. Before buying a home together, contact an attorney to discuss what legal issues you need to consider as an unmarried couple.
2. Consider keeping your assets and liabilities separate. You may decide to open a joint bank account, with each contributing money to pay joint expenses if you live together.
3. Consult with an attorney about creating a cohabitation or prenuptial agreement that specifies your financial responsibilities and defines the assets you each bring into the relationship. These agreements can also detail financial support and how to distribute property in the event of death or breakup.

WHEN YOU'RE ESTATE PLANNING SOLO

Pay Attention Even If You Aren't Single Now

Estate planning is just as crucial for singles as it is for married couples—maybe even more important. If you never married, got divorced, or are widowed, you may have different estate planning needs than married family members and friends.

If you're married, don't skip over this topic. In the future, you or someone you love may be in the position of being solo when it comes to creating or updating an estate plan.

ESTATE PLANNING CONSIDERATIONS

There are two significant issues to address when estate planning as a single person.

1. Who can take care of you and your property if you have a severe injury or illness or become incapacitated?
2. Who's to receive your property when you pass away, and how will your estate be handled?

Let's look at why these are essential questions for solo adults to answer and the estate planning tools that address them.

Who Will Care for You?

When you're married, your spouse is usually the person involved in your medical treatment and who makes medical decisions if you're unable to do so. They also typically take care of your personal property and manage finances on your behalf. But single people need to put a plan in place that gives someone they trust the legal authority to do those things. This is accomplished by:

1. Filling out a HIPAA authorization permitting a healthcare provider to share information with a person you designate.
2. Executing financial and healthcare powers of attorney (POAs).
3. Completing an advance healthcare directive.

As explained in Chapter 3, a POA document allows you to name an agent to legally act on your behalf. Depending on how you draft it and where you live, a financial POA can take effect at signing. Or you can have it only come into force if you become incapacitated. Make sure to understand the POA you're creating and the power it affords your agent.

Your medical POA is used only in the case of incapacitation. It's part of your advance directive, which also includes your living will. A living will provides crucial information about your medical wishes, such as the performance of life-sustaining measures, organ donation, and more. It's an essential form to have if you're single and may not have anyone to speak up for you in a crisis.

When you're single, you can choose parents, adult children, siblings, or other close relatives or friends as your agents. Who you designate for these critical positions depends on your circumstances, needs, and goals.

You may be considering one person to act as both your financial and medical POA. While that can work, make sure the person agrees to serve in these capacities and has the skills necessary to carry out each role. Don't forget to name an alternate agent if the original person you named refuses to or can no longer act on your behalf.

If you don't have anyone to serve in these roles, you have other options. You can hire a professional fiduciary from a bank or trust company to handle your financial affairs. Your attorney, doctor, or a local eldercare manager may have suggestions if you need a medical POA. If you don't have a healthcare agent, your living will should guide necessary healthcare decisions when you're unable to make them yourself.

Can My Doctor Be My Medical POA?

In most states, your agent can be any competent adult except your physician or healthcare provider (and employees of that provider), or a residential healthcare provider (nursing home) and employees. Relatives employed by these providers may be an exception.

A court will appoint others to manage your finances and make healthcare decisions for you (explained in a later section) if you become incapacitated without protections in place.

A HIPAA form, financial and medical POAs, and an advance directive should be on a single's to-do list. They give you the most control possible in managing your assets and health when you're in a critical medical situation.

Who Will Handle Your Estate?

A surviving spouse and children generally receive all or most of a deceased spouse's estate according to instructions left in a will or trust. When you're solo, you must create a will at a minimum. This avoids a court appointing a representative for you, a guardian for your children, and distributing your assets by intestate succession laws.

Keep in mind that without proper estate planning documents, a judge may distribute your property to children, parents, siblings, or even distant relatives against your wishes. And someone you may not have chosen could take guardianship of your children.

In creating your will or living trust, you'll choose a representative for your estate or a successor trustee. If you have minor children, you'll name a guardian for them too. While these may be the same people you named on other estate planning documents, it's again important to consider who has the time and skills to manage your estate. When in doubt, a bank or trust company can also take over much of your estate work.

You also have to decide who receives your property and business interests. If you have children or grandchildren, you can leave your assets to them. (If you plan to disinherit children, make sure you discuss how to do that legally with an attorney.)

You may also decide to divide up assets between relatives, friends, and favorite charities, and even leave funds for the care of your pet. Trusts are a good option for single people who want to maintain some control of their assets even after they die. Your attorney can help you decide whether a will, a trust—or both—will help you meet estate planning goals.

With proper planning, single adults have many options. You can design an estate plan that not only protects you but also supports the people and causes that matter most. The bottom line is making sure you have an updated estate plan in place that always reflects your wishes.

WHEN YOU HAVE A DEPENDENT WITH SPECIAL NEEDS

An Urgent "Must Do" to Protect a Loved One

Executing basic estate planning paperwork is essential for everyone. But when you have a family member with special needs, it's a must. You aren't just planning to protect yourself and your loved one's future; you must also prepare for a lifetime of care for your dependent.

PLANNING

While every family's circumstances are unique, there are layers of challenges to consider regarding special needs and estate planning. Your planning may include:

- Defining your vision for the life of your dependent with special needs
- Setting up legal and financial protections that preserve a dependent's eligibility for means-tested government benefits such as Medicaid and Supplemental Security Income (SSI)
- Naming a trustee to manage the dependent's finances
- Providing financially to enhance the quality of life for your dependent while you're alive and after your death
- Choosing a guardian or caretaker for your dependent

- Ensuring proper caregiving and providing financial resources (if possible) for when you're no longer able to manage their care
- Balancing the needs of other children and beneficiaries

Relocating?

Keep in mind that government benefits vary by state. The decision to move may impact your estate plan if your dependent with special needs receives different services in your new state of residence.

ESTATE PLANNING OPTIONS

There are a variety of choices to think through when addressing the previous challenges. But you should begin by spending time considering the future needs—physical, social, emotional, and financial—of your loved one with disabilities. And once you've determined their needs, you can start designing an estate plan to support them.

Before you think about drafting a will using one of the following options, consider the disadvantages discussed carefully. Following these choices are a couple of alternatives that could offer more benefits for you and your loved one.

Leave the Dependent an Inheritance

Leaving even a modest inheritance for your dependent with special needs increases the chances they'll become ineligible for or face a reduction in government benefits. When SSI and Medicaid are removed or reduced, your dependent may also become ineligible for a wide variety of essential services. These include assisted housing, home-delivered meals, education and training, employment assistance, transportation, personal care aides, and more.

Intentionally Disinherit the Dependent

Intentionally disinheriting the child is an option that may allow them to maintain government benefits. Still, it doesn't address how to finance any enhancements to the dependent's life quality. While it may not offer much help, it might be a better option than dying without a will. In that case, your dependent may inherit assets through intestate succession and lose government benefits.

Leave the Dependent's Inheritance to Siblings or Other Relatives

It may be a risky move, but you could leave the dependent's inheritance to a family member with the agreement to use the funds to care for the dependent. But if the individual doesn't follow your wishes or the assets end up in the wrong hands due to a divorce or poor money management, your dependent may not benefit from the inheritance.

When you have a dependent with a disability, you likely need more than just a last will and testament. In addition to your POAs and living will, comprehensive estate planning may include a letter of intent (LOI), a special needs trust (SNT), and an ABLE account.

Letter of Intent

You prepare a letter of intent (LOI) to educate a new guardian or caregiver so they can better understand, provide, and advocate for your loved one. In addition to being an essential guide to basic caregiving needs, this letter helps them learn about the pertinent laws, resources, and programs that benefit your dependent.

Your LOI may include your hopes about their future, a family history, and thoughts about their final arrangements. It can also discuss your dependent's likes and dislikes, along with their routines. You'll want to include their medical care, educational history, employment guidance, benefits received, religious preferences, social interests, and behavior management as well.

Will Option

Even if you don't include your heir with special needs in your last will and testament, you can name their guardian in your will.

Special Needs Trust

A special needs trust (SNT) addresses the shortcomings of using a will to provide an inheritance to a dependent with special needs. Since your dependent doesn't own the property in the trust, they should maintain needs-based government benefit eligibility.

SNT distributions don't give beneficiaries cash but instead provide for services and items not covered by government benefits. Qualifying expenses could include educational opportunities, hobbies, vacations, or funding the care of a pet.

You may choose a trust company or financial institution to serve as the trustee (or co-trustee with a family member) to manage assets and pay expenses. This helps protect your loved one from a family member using the funds for their care for another purpose.

Creating and implementing a trust is a complicated task. We strongly suggest working with a financial professional and estate planning attorney who has extensive experience drafting this type of trust.

ABLE Account

It should come as no surprise that people with disabilities have expenses not covered by government benefits. Yet, they have few options to grow savings to cover additional out-of-pocket costs that don't impact qualifying for public services.

With the passage of the Achieving a Better Life Experience Act of 2014 (aka ABLE Act), eligible individuals with disabilities can be beneficiaries of a particular tax-advantaged savings account. Family, friends, and the account beneficiary can contribute to the current tax law's annual limit. To be eligible for an ABLE account, the onset of one's disability must occur before age twenty-six.

Distributions from the account are tax-free to the beneficiary and can pay for various qualified disability expenses. The IRS defines these costs, including housing, education, transportation, health and wellness, employment training, assistive technology, and personal support services.

Along with being easier and less expensive to establish, these accounts can offer more flexibility than an SNT for the beneficiary and their family. You can learn more about these accounts on IRS.gov by searching for "ABLE Accounts: Tax Benefit for People with Disabilities."

CHOOSING TO DISINHERIT (OR NOT)

You Might Reconsider Leaving Them Out Completely

One of your primary goals in estate planning is determining who inherits your assets. It may be an easy decision for some people, but others struggle to include certain heirs. The disinheritance of a spouse, partner, child, or stepchild is more common than you might think. But disinheriting someone isn't as easy as only leaving them out of your will or trust. Heirs who have "standing" can challenge legal paperwork after your death and may win the right to receive a portion of your estate.

While you may have good reasons to disinherit someone, keep in mind that you won't be around to witness the results of this decision. Disinheritance can cause highly emotional conflicts and create even greater division between family members. That's why it's essential to understand what it means to disinherit someone. You need to understand who you can disinherit and why. Alternatives to disinheritance and steps to take when deciding to leave someone out of your will are also important to know.

DEFINING DISINHERITANCE

When you leave an heir out of estate planning documents, you disinherit them. And disinheritance can happen accidentally for a variety of reasons. But you may also want to intentionally prevent an heir from receiving any part of your estate.

Accidental disinheritance can result from failing to update your will after having a baby or getting remarried. Selling an asset that you left to an heir in your will could leave them without anything when you pass away. To prevent unintentional disinheritance, always review your estate plan after major life events and at least every few years.

While you may want to disinherit an heir purposely, laws in your state may prevent you from doing so. Let's look at who people attempt to disinherit and whether it's legal to do so.

Can You Disinherit a Spouse?

In general, you can't intentionally disinherit a spouse unless a valid prenuptial or postnuptial agreement is in place. A spouse can legally disinherit a surviving spouse by not passing them the property they brought into the marriage (separate property) as designated in the marital agreement.

Legally recognized domestic partners generally have the same inheritance rights as surviving spouses. Although state laws vary widely, a disinherited spouse without a marital agreement usually receives a portion of a deceased spouse's estate. In most states, surviving spouses are protected from total disinheritance by elective share law.

Elective share rights also vary. Some states allow a disinherited spouse to elect to take a portion of the deceased spouse's probate and non-probate assets, along with titled property. Others restrict this to the probate estate and just some non-probate assets.

But a majority of states that use elective share law only allow a disinherited spouse to take a portion of the probate estate. And if an estate is set up to avoid probate, a spouse may end up with no inheritance.

In a "community property" state, the surviving spouse generally receives at least half of the community property (all property the couple owns together) when the first spouse passes away. Before a spouse dies, they can choose to leave their half to their surviving spouse or other named beneficiaries.

What about Disinheriting Kids?

Adult children generally do not have any rights to inherit a portion of your estate. But minor children have different rights that protect their interests.

Whether you should disinherit an adult child is a difficult question to answer. There may be various reasons why you're considering cutting off a child from receiving financial assets after your death. You may be estranged from them, they may display ongoing irresponsible behaviors, or you may have already provided for them substantially as an adult. But if you're questioning whether to disinherit a child, you might think again and seek counsel from your attorney.

Disinheriting children is a powerful message and one that can affect them for the rest of their lives. Keep in mind that it may also impact more than just the child you disinherit. If they contest your will or trust, it can further damage any relationship they have with siblings and other family members.

Don't DIY a Disinheritance

If you plan to disinherit a child, don't just leave their name out of your will. Work with your attorney to determine the language needed in your paperwork to make the disinheritance valid. Otherwise, your child could still be awarded a portion of your estate.

You might consider an alternative to disinheritance before writing them off completely. Your attorney may suggest giving smaller gifts to an adult child rather than totally disinheriting them. Another option is adding a "no contest" clause to your estate planning documents to encourage a child to accept what you've left them.

Setting up a trust with a third-party trustee is another way to structure your estate, so you control the timing and amount of distributions to an adult child. You could also adjust a beneficiary designation to leave a small percentage of an asset to this heir. A disgruntled child may be less likely to challenge your estate and cause more family drama if you include them in at least some manner.

IF YOU DECIDE TO DISINHERIT

If you intentionally leave someone out of your will, make sure those you leave behind won't be left fighting with the one you disinherit. It's your job to prepare ahead to prevent an heir from challenging your will or trust.

You may decide to leave a letter of disinheritance explaining why you made specific decisions in your estate plan. It may be a challenging letter to write or for your heirs to read. But it can detail why individual gifts were made and explain any disparities between inheritances to beneficiaries. You can also suggest how to use gifts and add other sentiments that don't belong in a will.

While it may seem extreme, in some circumstances, an attorney might suggest having a medical evaluation to prove your competence when creating your estate plan. They might also recommend an independent review of your plan, so you have more witnesses backing up your decisions.

PLANNING FOR YOUR PETS

Caring for Fido When You're Gone

Creating an estate plan protects you and provides for those who matter most. But an often-overlooked family member in estate planning is the family pet or pets. Few pet owners make arrangements for their pets who may outlive them.

You might have talked informally with family or friends about who would care for Fido or Whiskers if something happened to you. But there are steps you can take to support your pet and their new caregiver.

PLANNING

Our pets provide unconditional love, but they also depend on our care. So, it's important to be proactive and think about how you want your pet to be taken care of and who can provide that care. Don't forget about planning how to pay for your pet's expenses too.

Consider Your Pet's Future Care

You know how to best care for your pet. That's why you should leave a written pet care plan or letter of instruction for a future caregiver. The plan should include typical daily routines for feeding (including food brand and amount), exercise, grooming, play, and sleep. Don't forget to share details about how well your pet gets along with other animals and children, as well as any behavioral challenges.

Intestate Laws Apply to Pets Too

If you haven't made plans for your pet and you die without a will, your state's intestate succession laws determine who gets your pet. A relative may agree to it (even if they can't afford it), but it might not be who you would have chosen.

You should also provide your veterinarian's contact information and consent for the caregiver to authorize treatment for your pet. While the caregiver will make the final decisions, you can also include your wishes regarding a severe illness or injury and final arrangements for your pet.

If you have more than one pet, each should have an individual care plan. You can give a copy of the plans to your relatives or friends who may serve as caregivers, along with your attorney and veterinarian.

Determine Possible Pet Guardians

You may have someone in mind to care for your pet when you no longer can, but make sure the person agrees to take on the responsibility for your pet. You can share the pet care plan you created and see if it raises any red flags with the potential guardian. It's essential to have more than one potential caregiver if someone is unable or unwilling to care for your pet.

If you have no family members or friends to fill this role, you can contact your local humane society and ask if they rehome pets for someone who has passed away.

Calculate Annual Pet Expenses

To provide financial support for your pet and its caregiver, you need to figure out how much you spend on your pet yearly. Your estimate should include food, veterinary care, medications, grooming, and boarding costs. You may have other pet expenses, including treats and toys, training classes, or pet daycare.

By knowing the annual expenses and your pet's life expectancy, you can determine how much money you want to provide to fund your pet's care. To avoid challenges by your heirs, make sure the amount of money you leave for your pet's care is reasonable.

If You Have a Rescue

You might need to follow a rescue organization's guidelines for creating a pet care plan if you adopted your pet. Some organizations have restrictions on caregivers and where pets can go when you can no longer provide care.

FORMALIZING YOUR PLAN

By completing the previous steps, you've already made progress in terms of safeguarding your pet's future. Even if you decide an informal agreement is all that's needed, your pet's caretaker will appreciate the information compiled about your pet. But some people prefer creating a legally enforceable agreement to help ensure others follow their wishes.

There are several ways to accomplish this, such as accounting for your pet in your will, including pet provisions in your living trust, or establishing a freestanding pet trust.

Including Your Pet in Your Will

Like other property in your will, you can specify a beneficiary to take ownership of your pet and money for the beneficiary to care for your pet. You can also name alternate beneficiaries or organizations to care for your pet and leave money for them.

But keep in mind that the pet's guardian isn't usually accountable for spending the money as you directed. Will assets for pet care can only be used upon your death; they don't apply for incapacitation cases.

Adding Pet Provisions to a Comprehensive Living Trust

With a living trust, you can add a provision identifying your pet's caretaker and how you'll fund your pet's care. You can also name an alternate caretaker or organization.

This option's downsides are that your pet's caretaker may not use the funds as you directed. They also aren't able to access more money to care for your pet if needed.

Creating a Stand-Alone Pet Trust

This type of trust is more complex and usually costs more to create, but it's established explicitly for your pet and their care. Since you make this outside of your will, it's useful if you're incapacitated.

You'll need a trustee to administer a pet trust, and while it may be the pet's caretaker, you can also name someone else as the trustee. The trustee will then be in charge of providing funds to the pet's guardian.

After your pet dies, your trust will also direct where any remaining funds go. You may decide to give your pet's caretaker money or direct it to an animal-focused charity.

WHEN INCAPACITY OR EMERGENCY ISSUES ARISE

Plan Ahead to Avoid Additional Crises

We've repeatedly stressed the importance of having a will at a minimum in your estate plan. By now, it should be clear that without a will or living trust, your state intestacy laws determine what happens to your property—perhaps the guardianship of your children too.

We've also discussed the need for POAs and advance care directives to ensure someone can handle your health and financial matters if you're unable to do so yourself. What we haven't discussed in detail is what happens when you haven't drawn up this paperwork and incapacitation becomes an issue.

UNDERSTANDING LEGAL INCAPACITY

It shouldn't be a surprise that POAs grow in importance as people get older due to age-related illnesses such as Alzheimer's and dementia. But there's a real possibility an accident or sudden illness could leave anyone, young or old, in a state of incapacity. When a person cannot perform essential requirements for their physical health, safety, or care, they may be deemed incapacitated. This may include a temporary or permanent inability to make decisions, manage finances, or attend to medical care due to a mental or physical disability or illness.

Whether the circumstances causing incapacity arise with some degree of warning or in one terrible instant, someone must be appointed to make financial and health-related decisions for the legally incapacitated person. When you create estate plan documents, you get to choose those agents. When you don't, the court appoints a guardian and conservator for you.

When You Plan

By establishing power of attorney and advance care directives as described in Chapter 3, you can provide instructions for your medical care and treatment and your financial matters. You can also appoint someone to ensure your instructions are followed and give them the ability to make other healthcare decisions for you.

Having these forms in place makes certain your wishes are known if your health deteriorates or a sudden emergency puts you in a dire situation. It also removes the burden from loved ones trying to determine what you'd want in a debilitating, disabling, or life-threatening condition while emotionally adjusting to your new circumstances.

When No Legal Documents Exist

A competent individual must create POAs, wills, and other legal forms before incapacitation. When you're already incapacitated, it's too late for you to make them.

Suppose you become physically or mentally incapacitated or otherwise unable to make your own decisions in healthcare or financial matters without POAs. In that case, legal proceedings become necessary to give someone else the authority to manage your affairs.

While the specifics may vary by state, your ability to manage your health and welfare is challenged during court proceedings for guardianship (aka conservatorship of the person). The legal proceeding to establish an inability to take care of your financial estate is called a conservatorship (aka guardian of the estate). Some states use only the term *guardianship* for both.

If you are proven to be incapacitated through the court, which typically requires medical evidence, your rights are taken away, and you become a "protected person." The judge appoints a guardian as the decision-maker in your health and welfare matters. At the same time, they may assign a conservator to manage and protect your estate. One individual may occupy both roles, or separate people can be chosen for each position. The judge could also appoint two individuals to a role as co-conservators or co-guardians.

How Are Proceedings Started?

A family member often brings a petition, but anyone concerned about another's welfare can file a petition for guardianship or conservatorship. Someone could also challenge an existing POA by filing for guardianship/conservatorship if they feel the agent cannot act in the incapacitated person's best interests.

The court will follow their state's laws when determining a person's incompetence and naming a guardian and/or conservator. When more than one family member or friend petitions for either role, the judge follows state law preferences. Preference usually goes to spouses, parents, adult children or siblings, or other close relatives. Unmarried partners may not be given priority over blood relatives, which could cause heartache and strain relationships. When no one is available (or appropriate) for the role of guardian or conservator, the judge may appoint a professional.

Can Proceedings Be Challenged?

Anyone whose competence is challenged has the right to appear in court and object to a petition with an attorney's help. The court will appoint an attorney to them, if necessary.

Anyone else objecting to the petition or the individual filing a petition can attend the hearing to raise concerns to the judge. They must file papers with the court, inform all interested parties, and attend the proceedings if they want to legally contest or block a guardianship.

What a Guardian and Conservator Do

An appointed guardian makes welfare choices for a protected person. This includes their living arrangements, medical and health-care needs, and other general safety and long-term care needs. There may be limits on the decisions guardians can make without court approval in some states or cases.

Guardians assume responsibility for supplying food, clothing, and personal necessities and ensuring proper care, maintenance, and support. They become the healthcare contact and manage and authorize any medical and health-related appointments and care. Depending on state laws, a guardian may or may not have any financial responsibilities.

A conservator appointed by the court is assigned to manage the financial assets of a protected individual. This typically includes paying regular bills and expenses, managing investment accounts, selling or buying property, preparing and filing tax returns, and other financial-related requirements. Some states may limit responsibilities or require court approval before specific actions can be carried out.

Conservators must account for all financial transactions performed. Many states require filing financial inventories and annual reporting of the estate's finances.

Protecting the Estate

Depending on an estate's size, the court may order a conservator to secure a bond, or the court may restrict the amount of money a conservator has access to at one time.

Termination of a Conservatorship or Guardianship

The responsibilities of a guardian and conservator automatically end at the death of a protected person. An accounting of assets and a final hearing are typically required to close the case.

When a protected person is no longer incapacitated, they may file a petition with the court to remove a conservator and guardian. This typically requires reports from one or more doctors attesting to the person's competence.

Someone can petition to remove an appointed guardian or conservator when they suspect fiduciary obligations are not being met. A new petition for guardianship or conservatorship would need to be filed by someone willing to assume either role.

Be Proactive

To prevent the need for a conservatorship or guardianship, prepare POAs and advanced care directives. These, along with a will, are the essential elements of an estate plan. A living trust may also prove beneficial to protect and manage your estate if you cannot do so.

ESTATE PLANNING FOR ENTREPRENEURS AND FAMILY BUSINESSES

You Need a Succession Plan

Whether you're a solo entrepreneur, a partner in a small enterprise, or one of several owners in a family business, you have some additional steps to prepare a solid estate plan. Working with experienced legal and financial professionals is your best bet for ensuring all your needs are covered when you own a business. Here we'll discuss some things to think through before meeting with an estate planning attorney who has experience working with business owners.

CAN THE BUSINESS GO ON?

First, you need to honestly answer if the business could (or should) continue without you. Could someone step into your role? Would anyone want to? Could the company (or your share of it) be sold? Will it need to be sold to provide for your heirs?

A succession plan defines what happens when you no longer can or want to serve in your business leadership role. If you haven't already done succession planning, you should add it to your list of priorities. When planning for what would happen in a family business, you'll need to think about whether your spouse or children could or would want to take over the company. Or would it make more sense for them to own it with someone else managing it?

Next, you need to determine if and how the business would run until full execution of a succession plan. Do you have an individual or team in place to take over your responsibilities? Does the company have adequate finances to carry on until matters are settled? Are probate-avoidance measures in place to ensure funds are available?

Where a succession plan provides the blueprints for how a transfer of leadership and ownership should play out, a financial emergency plan offers the stability to help ensure it's carried out.

Even if your business is an owner-dependent operation and may end upon your passing, you should still address estate planning matters. For example, tax, insurance, risk, and other financial and legal planning measures need attention in any business to maximize profits and reduce professional and personal liability.

HOW DOES THE BUSINESS GO ON?

The size of your business and whether you share ownership or not guides much of the decision to end, continue, or sell the business. If you currently share business ownership, the first question to answer is if any legal documents that are in place control the disposition of ownership. Your plan cannot trump what corporate by-laws, LLC operating agreements, partnership agreements, or shareholder agreements say. Here are some other things you'll need to think through.

If your family keeps ownership:

- Who will have formal ownership?
- Will they have management powers or only a share of the profits?
- If only some of your children will have ownership, how can you provide fairly for others?

- Who assumes key leadership roles?
- How and when can they be trained to assume responsibilities?
- How can disputes among family members be resolved?
- If surviving co-owners exist:
  - What provisions are in place to cover surviving owner rights?
  - Do they have a "right" to buy out shares, or "must" they buy out shares?
  - If heirs can sell shares, do other owners have the "right of first refusal" before offering them to others?
  - How are payments made to heirs if surviving owners buy out shares?
  - What happens if heirs try to sell shares but cannot secure a buyer?
- Selling to others:
  - When would it make sense to sell the business?
  - How does it operate until sold?
  - How can a buyer be found?
  - Is selling to a key employee or several employees an option?
  - What about selling to a competitor or a supplier?

As you can see, there are several issues to consider. And no matter what ultimately happens to the business, providing for and treating your heirs fairly is probably of the utmost importance to you. Speak to trusted advisors who should have several ideas on how you can structure your succession plan.

What about Probate?

Generally, all assets, even business assets, go through probate unless probate avoidance measures, such as beneficiary designations, joint tenancy, or a living trust, are used.

BUSINESS ESTATE PLANNING

The need for essential elements of an estate plan—a will and POAs—are compounded when you're a business owner. Without a will, your company and heirs are at the mercy of state laws regarding the business's operation and division. And you'll need a financial POA to authorize someone to manage your company finances and perform business transactions in the event you're incapacitated. You'll likely need more than just the basics, however. A trust, estate tax planning, and additional life and disability insurance are other things to consider.

You may look to buy life and disability policies with your business as the beneficiary in terms of the insurance. This is in addition to policies you have with your family as beneficiary. These insurance policies, known as key (or critical) person insurance, can be highly beneficial to pay business expenses while the company goes through succession. Your accountant or financial advisor can help you determine the amount of coverage you should purchase.

You'll want to discuss any concerns about federal estate or state inheritance taxes with your financial professionals as well. They can also help you work with your estate planning attorney if you decide to set up a living trust or pursue other trust options.

You'll need to have discussions with family and any business partners as you do estate planning for your company to avoid unnecessary surprises and problems later. But once it's complete, make sure all key individuals know the plan and how to execute it when necessary. Also, be sure to keep it updated.

Chapter 8

Completing the Package

All the thinking, organizing, and list-making you do isn't an estate plan. You must create the legal paperwork to put your plan into play. Without drafting the forms, funding the trusts, instructing agents, and sharing the information with loved ones, your estate planning is incomplete. Even once you've completed those things, estate planning isn't over.

Time and events will mean reviewing your plan and making needed changes. Plus, there are other things you'll want family and friends to know. Some of these things, such as your insurance agent's contact info or the maintenance records for your home, will be best left in an informational notebook or a digital spreadsheet. Others are better suited for a personal letter.

AVOIDING COMMON MISTAKES

Tips for Getting It Right the First Time

An estate plan that's full of mistakes might cause more harm than good. Make sure you read all legal documents thoroughly and correct any errors you find before signing them. Misspelled names or incorrect addresses, accidentally omitting an heir, or gifting the wrong asset to a beneficiary can happen. While you can easily fix those types of mistakes when caught, they may cause lots of grief when they're not.

COMMON MISTAKES IN ESTATE PLANNING

Here is a list of frequent estate planning mistakes people make, followed by a checklist to use when doing yours. While neither is an exhaustive list, they can help you avoid errors and track necessary steps as you strategize and put your plan into play.

- **Not planning at all!** You're headed in the right direction by reading this book. Now you need to put in the work.
- **Planning but not implementing.** Without a will, power of attorney, and advance directives, your state determines who manages your affairs and how your property's distributed. To have your final wishes known and followed, create those legal forms at a minimum.
- **Not doing any other financial planning.** Estate planning is just one part of a more extensive financial planning process. Not putting time and effort into other areas could put your finances at risk.

- **Focusing too narrowly on individual assets.** Because specific items in your estate vary over time, consider leaving heirs a percentage of your estate's value instead of giving them assets individually. This eliminates the need to revise your will every time significant investments change.
- **Misunderstanding how assets are owned and/or passed upon death.** Jointly held property may pass differently than you expect. And some money (retirement accounts or life insurance) passes to beneficiaries outside of a will or trust. Be sure you understand how "what" goes to "who" when you die.
- **Not naming beneficiaries or listing them incorrectly.** Not designating a valid beneficiary or failing to remove one you no longer want to benefit after you die can put assets in the wrong hands.
- **Not providing contingent beneficiaries.** If a beneficiary's no longer living at your time of death, their benefit passes to a co- or contingent beneficiary. If neither is listed, the benefit becomes a part of your general estate and may not go to someone you'd otherwise choose.
- **Stopping at a will (or a trust).** A will alone is not an estate plan. Be sure to establish power of attorneys and advance directives and consider your need for a trust, now and in the future. Likewise, a trust alone may not meet all the needs of your estate. The combination of a will and trust may provide the best protection.
- **Not correctly funding a trust.** You must transfer assets to a trust for your estate to receive the trust's benefits.
- **Failing to plan for incapacity.** While it may be difficult to imagine being unable to communicate or manage your medical and financial affairs, creating POAs before possible incapacitation will be much easier on everyone than obtaining an emergency guardianship and conservatorship later.

- **Forgetting about taxes.** Be sure you consider the tax conse-quences (for you and your beneficiaries) of any actions you take in your planning.
- **Losing control of assets.** Adding someone to your bank account or giving them partial ownership of your property could put you at risk of losing those assets due to their mishandling of your funds. You could also be unintentionally creating a gift tax situa-tion or reducing potential benefits you could use later.
- **Not designating a property guardian to manage assets left to minors.** When you don't name a guardian in your will, the court intervenes. Assets are turned over to your children when they turn eighteen (often not a good combination!).
- **Forgetting about pets.** With no plan in place for your pets' care, they could end up spending the rest of their lives in a shelter.
- **Creating a DIY plan without any legal assistance.** Trying to cut costs by going the DIY route or using an attorney who doesn't specialize in estate planning can cost you more in the long run. If you must DIY your plan, see if you can pay for legal advice or a plan review with a lawyer familiar with estate plans.
- **Failing to provide protections for an heir with special needs.** The best place for assets you want to leave for the benefit of a loved one with a disability is in a special needs trust. An SNT helps you provide for them without putting their ability to receive government assistance at risk.
- **Not making changes when divorcing.** As soon as you or a spouse files for a divorce, take steps to amend your estate plan. If you don't, the control of your assets could still go to your spouse if something were to happen to you. Be sure to change beneficiary designations too.
- **Failing to make changes after remarriage.** Update estate plan paperwork and assets with beneficiary designations to include

your new spouse. Additionally, if you and your new spouse have children from prior relationships, put protections in place for not only each other but each other's children too.

- **Not discussing the plan with others.** Keeping your goals and plans private can cause unintended hurt feelings and confusion, from how you split assets to how you wanted your trust managed.
- **Not keeping proper records.** Your agents, representatives, trustees, heirs, beneficiaries, and other loved ones will need more details than your legal documents alone may provide. Maintain a detailed list of assets, liabilities, insurance policies, and other vital records so others have information to handle your affairs when you no longer can.
- **Failing to review and update financial and estate plans.** Because we experience life changes often, an annual planning review is wise. It's a chance to revisit your goals, address new needs, implement changes due to the tax code or estate laws, and make updates to beneficiaries, trusts, and more.

Estate Planning Checklist

Use this checklist when doing your planning—even when working with an attorney—to help ensure you're covering all your bases.

- ❏ Establish goals
- ❏ Inventory assets
- ❏ Inventory liabilities
- ❏ Inventory digital assets, profiles, and passwords
- ❏ Evaluate disability insurance needs and purchase a policy
- ❏ Evaluate life insurance needs and buy a policy

- ❏ Designate beneficiaries or transfer on death/payable on death for:
    - ❏ Life insurance
    - ❏ IRAs
    - ❏ 401(k)
    - ❏ Bank accounts
    - ❏ Investment accounts
    - ❏ Stocks
    - ❏ Bonds
- ❏ Create a living will/advance care directives (medical power of attorney)
- ❏ Obtain general financial power of attorney
- ❏ Draft will
- ❏ Create living trust if applicable
- ❏ Fund living trust if applicable
- ❏ Consider lifetime gifting strategy
- ❏ Consider donor-advised fund and/or charitable remainder trust
- ❏ Create a business succession plan
- ❏ Plan for long-term care
- ❏ Plan for end-of-life and funeral arrangements and establish funds to pay for them
- ❏ Write letters of instruction for personal representatives, guardians, and trustees
- ❏ Write letters to family and friends
- ❏ Assemble an emergency binder
- ❏ Secure originals and safely store copies, and provide to others as needed
- ❏ Set up calendar dates for ongoing review and management of the plan

WHAT ELSE THEY'LL NEED TO KNOW

In Case of Emergency Information

We know we cannot control when we'll die or if and when we could become incapacitated. But we can control how well we prepare to help our family and loved ones through an emergency when we're hurt, ill, or no longer here. The thought of recording all they'll need to know may seem daunting, but it'll be incredibly helpful to them in case of an emergency.

EMERGENCY BINDER OR DIGITAL NOTEBOOK

Much of the information you'll gather checks the boxes on your estate planning to-do list too. You can find templates and resources at http://womenwhomoney.com/estate-planning-tools to help organize the information and keep it safe. But any notebook and paper or spreadsheet can do to start. What's most important is getting all your paperwork and details together. You may decide to create more than one notebook, keeping confidential information locked up with only a few having access. A later section of this chapter addresses document storage and accessibility.

This list may be long, but not all of it will apply to you. And chances are it won't take as long to collect the information as you might fear. You can enlist the help of others too. The goal of collecting this information is to provide you and your family with the tools to pick up the pieces and move on when life events interrupt daily living.

Ideas for What to Include

The detail level is up to you, and while there is a chance you could provide too many details, that probably won't happen. You might adopt the concept of "beginner's mind" and remember that whoever is seeking the information may not know precisely what to do with it. Even if they might know, things are different at times of grief and stress; both big and small details get overlooked or forgotten altogether. Think of your emergency notebook as a gift to loved ones: a practical guide for going on during a crisis or after a loss.

Bonus!

Physical or digital notebooks with vital information can be at your fingertips (or accessible in the cloud) if you ever need to leave home quickly in an emergency. You know this is important to do, and you can see how useful it would be to others. You also know it could take some time to do it. Make the time by setting aside a few minutes each day, or get it all done next weekend. You could also see if your book club, moms' group, or best friends want to do this too. Then motivate and hold each other accountable until you complete them.

The final step is telling your most trusted family or friends about your plan and where they can find the information, if and when they'll need it.

EMERGENCY INFORMATION CHECKLIST

For anyone new to the idea of creating an emergency preparedness binder for your family, this list will get you going quickly.

Important Contact Names and Phone Numbers

- ❏ Emergency numbers for utility companies
- ❏ Family and friends
- ❏ Kids' schools and daycare providers
- ❏ Doctors, dentists, and hospitals/clinics
- ❏ Clergy/religious leaders
- ❏ Work and business associates
- ❏ Local non-emergency numbers for police, fire, ambulance, and city
- ❏ Funeral home
- ❏ Military services

Personal Details (for Each Family Member)

- ❏ Full name, date of birth, and Social Security number
- ❏ Up-to-date photo
- ❏ Current employment/school details
- ❏ Copies of vital documents
    - ❏ Driver's licenses or state-issued ID cards
    - ❏ Social Security cards
    - ❏ Credit cards (front and back)
    - ❏ Military records
    - ❏ Adoption/foster records
    - ❏ Naturalization/immigration papers
    - ❏ Religious records

- ❏ Medical information
  - ❏ Advanced care directives
  - ❏ Medical power of attorney
  - ❏ Immunization records
  - ❏ Medical history if you have serious illnesses/diseases
  - ❏ Current prescription lists
  - ❏ Insurance information—copies of your cards (front and back)
- ❏ Children
  - ❏ School details
  - ❏ Activities/routines
  - ❏ Close friends' names and parent contact info
  - ❏ Likes/dislikes
- ❏ Pets
  - ❏ Name, breed, date of birth
  - ❏ Veterinary info
  - ❏ Medical history and prescription details
  - ❏ Insurance info
  - ❏ Routine

Household

- ❏ Homeowners insurance company/agent contact
- ❏ Home maintenance and repair information
- ❏ Contact details for service people
- ❏ Home inventory
- ❏ Utility company names and contact info
- ❏ Spare keys/security info
- ❏ Addresses and details of storage facilities
- ❏ (Repeat for vacation homes/other real property)

Vehicles

- ❏ Auto insurance company/agent contact
- ❏ Copy of proof of insurance and registration
- ❏ Maintenance and repair information
- ❏ Contact details for sales and service providers
- ❏ Spare keys/security info
- ❏ (Repeat for each vehicle)

Financial Information

- ❏ Banking
  - ❏ Branch location/contact/phone numbers
  - ❏ Savings and checking account numbers
  - ❏ Debit and credit card numbers
  - ❏ Auto deposit and bill pay info
  - ❏ Website, username, and passwords
  - ❏ Recent statement
- ❏ Credit cards
  - ❏ Issuers and contact details
  - ❏ Card account numbers
  - ❏ Website, username, and passwords
- ❏ Mortgage
  - ❏ Provider and contact details
  - ❏ Account number and payment details
  - ❏ Website, username, and passwords
- ❏ Other loans
  - ❏ Providers' contact info
  - ❏ Account numbers and payment details
  - ❏ Websites, usernames, and passwords
- ❏ Insurance
  - ❏ Company/agent details

- ❏ Policy numbers, basics on coverage, deductibles
- ❏ Website, username, and passwords
- ❏ Investment and retirement accounts
  - ❏ Financial institutions and phone numbers
  - ❏ Type of account (401[k], Roth or traditional IRA, brokerage)
  - ❏ Account numbers
  - ❏ Auto-investment option details
  - ❏ Website, username, and passwords
  - ❏ Recent statements
- ❏ Copy of last two years' tax returns (or location details of originals)
- ❏ Monthly/annual income and expense information
- ❏ Utility company payment details: account numbers, website, username, and passwords
- ❏ Cash for use in an emergency

Legal Documents

If desired, keep originals secure and copies in your notebook.

- ❏ Power of attorney for you
- ❏ Power of attorney for others—if you're someone else's agent
- ❏ Will
- ❏ Deed and titles to your real estate, cars, and other motor vehicles
- ❏ Birth certificates—you can order duplicate official certificates from your state agencies
- ❏ Wedding licenses
- ❏ Passports
- ❏ Lease information
- ❏ Divorce decrees
- ❏ Death certificates

Digital Profiles and Passwords

❏ Email accounts
❏ Social media accounts
❏ Online forums
❏ Memberships: Amazon Prime, Apple, Hulu, Netflix, cloud storage, etc.

Business

While you should have an emergency notebook specific for your business, providing some details can be beneficial.

❏ Legal documents (copies)
❏ Banking/financial information
❏ Important associates to contact
❏ Website management info
❏ Email account usernames and passwords
❏ Spare keys/security access info

Legacy/Other

❏ Letters of instruction
❏ Letters to family and friends
❏ Memorial service wishes
❏ Genealogy/ancestry/family tree info

LETTERS AND LEGACY

Gifts from the Heart

In the last section of Chapter 2 ("Leaving a Legacy Behind"), we introduced legacy planning and the idea of leaving behind more than financial gifts. This section presents questions and thought experiments to help you think further about how you're living today and how you want others to remember you tomorrow. Set aside time to do the exercises—and grab some paper and a pen.

BEGIN WITH THE END IN MIND

Before going anywhere, we must have a destination in mind. Knowing a physical address or imagining a visual concept can help us plan a route to get from here to there. When we don't know where we're going, we won't have a direction to head, milestones to measure progress, or a reason for arriving.

Focus Forward

"Begin with the end in mind" is habit number two from *The 7 Habits of Highly Effective People*, by Stephen Covey. It's based on the principle that all things are created first mentally and then physically. Consciously visualizing who you are and what you want in life empowers you and not others to shape your life.

As challenging as it is to imagine your last days on earth and what happens next, it can help you understand how daily life choices create the legacy you leave behind forty, sixty, or eighty years from now.

Answer the questions here to begin thinking about how the end of your life might look; take notes to capture your thoughts.

- You have two years to live. What would you do in that time and why?
- If you had only six months to live, would your answer change? Why?
- What would you regret most if today or tomorrow was your last day alive?
- Imagine your funeral. What are people saying about you? Is it what you'd like them to say? If not, what do you wish they were saying?

Past, Present, Future

Thinking about your legacy can bring up an abundance of emotions as you evaluate the past, analyze where you are today, and make plans for the future. Taking a mental inventory of your accomplishments, disappointments, family, estate, career, and things you've done or left undone can be equally uplifting and sobering. It can also be exhausting. But the effort you put into it can also be gratifying when done.

Consider the following questions as you reflect on the past and present and visualize the future.

- What do you stand for?
- How do you want your inner circle of family and friends to remember you?
- What will those beyond your inner circle remember you for?
- What work or business contributions do you want to make to your field?

- What community impacts will you make?
- How will your place in the world make it better for others?
- Whose lives have you touched?
- What lessons do you hope to pass on to future generations?
- What gifts do you want to leave to others?

WHAT WILL YOUR LEGACY BE?

Now we suggest writing your obituary—the one you want others to publish after your death. There's no right or wrong way to do this. Some obituaries are brief, while others include numerous family members, education and work histories, career and life accomplishments, interests and hobbies, and more. Here is a list of details you might want to include:

- Who you were personally and professionally
- The special people in your life—who they were, and what you meant to each other
- Other people or causes you affected
- Major life accomplishments
- The values and traits you're known for
- Your hobbies, interests, and passions
- The legacy you leave behind

Who Are You Today?

This list of questions can help determine if how you're living today is moving you toward the person you want to be—the person you wrote about in the previous exercise.

In other words, you should be able to determine if you're currently spending your time, money, and attention in alignment with your vision of yourself and how you want others to remember you.

- What are your passions?
- What motivates or inspires you?
- What are your values, and how are you honoring them?
- How do you like to spend your time?
- Are you making a difference?
- What makes you happy?
- What is essential in your life?
- How do you treat others?

Living Your Legacy

You get to define your legacy, not someone else. In fact, you're adding to your legacy every day. But are you adding the things you want?

- Is who you are today pointing you in the right direction?
- Will you achieve the legacy you envision if you stay on your current path? If not, what changes will you need to make to leave behind the legacy you desire?
- What do you need to do to live your legacy now? How do you need to spend your time, attention, and money?

BEHIND THE SCENES

While our legacy tells much of our story, what lies behind the story is important too. Some may even say it's more important.

You can share more of your story and your hopes and wishes for the future in "letters" to your loved ones. They can be written on paper, typed into a computer, recorded on a video or audio, as formally or informally as you desire. Just as there is no one way to create a legacy, there's no one way to leave private communication behind.

Your letters may tell stories about the most impactful people or experiences of your life and how they affected you. Or why you took specific chances and let others pass you by. What you hope the future holds and your best advice for living it. And perhaps most importantly, your letters to your family or closest friends are a chance to tell them one last time what they meant to you. They are a gift beyond your legacy that can impact them more than any money or possessions can.

For more ideas and inspiration, visit https://legacyproject.org.

PLANNING TO CLOSE YOUR DIGITAL ACCOUNTS

Shuttering Your Online Identity

You've made lists of your assets—both tangible and intangible—and created a plan to protect them during your lifetime and distribute them upon your death. But there's a possibility you've overlooked some of your other online accounts during the estate planning process.

As your digital footprint expands, it's essential to determine what should happen to all your electronic property and who should be in charge of it in case of incapacitation or death. This includes your email and social media accounts, along with digital subscriptions such as cloud-based storage.

You don't want to make the mistake of thinking your accounts will go inactive or get deleted when you pass away or can no longer manage them. While that may be the case with some, proactively planning for future management of these accounts and the data or property within them is best.

REVISED UNIFORM FIDUCIARY ACCESS TO DIGITAL ASSETS ACT OF 2015 (RUFADAA)

Recent legislation regarding online property (RUFADAA) has been adopted in some form by almost every state. It addresses providing your personal representative or agent (fiduciaries) with authority to manage your digital assets, including computer files, virtual currency, and financial accounts. RUFADAA also allows you to outline how you want electronic communications managed and disposed of in your estate plan.

When you're incapacitated or pass away, the fiduciaries designated in your plan don't get blanket access to your email, text messages, and social media accounts. RUFADAA determines whether they can access online communications based on the following (in descending order of authority):

1. Whether you've provided direction for giving a third party some level of access to your account in an "online tool" offered by a provider. These directives also supersede those in estate planning documents such as your will. For example, your best friend is your *Facebook* Legacy Contact. Your sister is the personal representative named in your will. In this case, your best friend will get limited access to manage your memorialized *Facebook* page.

2. If you've given access to your online property through estate planning documents such as a will, trust, or POA. Note: Include the extent of access you want to provide a fiduciary when adding digital assets in these documents. For example, you may wish to have your brother close out your email accounts, but you may not authorize him to access text messages.

3. Without any directives, the terms of service of the provider apply. Carefully consider what you want to happen with each of your digital accounts. Make sure you follow through on using online tools when available and document the level of fiduciary access you're comfortable with providing in your estate planning documents. This will allow your representatives to carry out your wishes legally.

Prevent Ghosting

Creating a plan that allows someone to manage your online accounts after your death can help prevent "ghosting," or the identity theft of a deceased person. Those in fiduciary roles can monitor your credit file and address concerns quickly, saving your family much stress during an already difficult time.

SORTING THROUGH ACCOUNTS

Let's look at common digital accounts and their policies regarding deceased users, accessing content, and closing accounts.

Email

You may have several email accounts from various providers. When you search how they handle a deceased person's (inactive) account, you'll notice that policies vary.

Gmail

Google allows you to set up an "inactive account manager" to provide information about who should have access to your account and when to delete it. If you fail to use that tool, loved ones or a fiduciary can contact Google, but they may not be able to do anything other than close the account.

Outlook

Microsoft's policy is that someone can close your account if they have your account credentials. If not, they don't want to be contacted, and they'll close the account automatically after two years of inactivity.

Yahoo!

There is no option to get passwords or content from a *Yahoo!* account unless the deceased left access to it. Closing a *Yahoo!* mail account without access requires a letter with your *Yahoo!* ID, a copy of a document appointing the requesting party as the personal representative or executor of your estate, and a copy of your death certificate.

Social Media and Social Network Accounts

Some people want to leave parts of their online life behind, but others are eager to erase their digital presence when they die. Whether you want someone to post a final message from you, let others know you've passed away, or neither, you need to understand the different platforms' policies. Here are a few examples:

Facebook

You can set up a Legacy Contact to manage your memorialized account. But removing your page requires documentation from immediate family or your representative, along with a copy of your death certificate. *Instagram*'s policies are similar but may not require as much documentation.

Twitter

Your fiduciary or family member can request that *Twitter* remove your account by providing specific documentation, including a copy of your identification and death certificate.

LinkedIn

A fiduciary can request the memorialization of your *LinkedIn* profile or the closing of the account. They'll have to provide a copy of a death certificate and legal documents showing their authority to act on your behalf.

Reddit

If you provide log-in information, someone can delete your account. Otherwise, they can message moderators from a separate account and provide evidence of your death to have the account reviewed and deleted.

Cloud-Based Storage

Many people have documents, photos, videos, or music in cloud-based storage. But the ability to access content and close accounts varies with each provider.

Dropbox

Someone else accessing your *Dropbox* account must provide documentation proving they have a legal right to access the files. According to *Dropbox*, "a valid court order establishing that it was the deceased person's intent that you have access to the files in their account after the person passed away, and that Dropbox is compelled by law to provide the deceased person's files to you." Be sure to include permissions for your fiduciaries in your estate planning documents.

iCloud

According to Apple, there are no rights of survivorship with your account. "Any rights to your Apple ID or Content within your account terminate upon your death." Deleting your account and all contents within will occur upon receipt of a copy of your death certificate.

There's plenty you can do to protect yourself and minimize the work for those in charge of managing your estate. To ensure your representatives and loved ones have access and legal protection in your state, make sure to discuss digital accounts with your estate planning attorney.

SHARING YOUR PLAN

The Importance of Communication

You now understand the basics of estate planning, and you've done the work to execute the essential elements. But you should keep in mind that the loved ones who will implement your plan may not have the same level of understanding as you do. You don't want trusted agents or family members to have to learn about and take action to fulfill their new duties as they grieve your loss.

Key players in your estate plan must understand their role and accept the position. That's why you need to continue communicating with them after your plan is complete. As time goes on and everyone's life circumstances change, you may need to make changes to your estate plan and those in fiduciary roles.

There are different ways to accomplish this, including having family meetings and leaving written letters that communicate your intentions. Your age, relationships, and personal circumstances may impact how you choose to share aspects of your estate plan.

FAMILY AND FIDUCIARY MEETINGS

One way to communicate and educate family and friends is to meet with them. You may choose to meet individually, but bringing this group together to hear the same message at the same time can encourage discussion, promote transparency, and minimize conflict.

Depending on your estate's complexity or family dynamics, you may decide to include your attorney in the discussion. Another option is to record questions and concerns that group members voice and discuss them with your attorney.

Goals of your meeting(s) may include:

- Sharing that estate documents are in place, their location, and who has access
- Discussing the role of each fiduciary (agents, executor, guardians, trustee)
- Explaining your expectations and reasons for your decisions
- Minimizing objections and misunderstandings
- Allowing family and friends to ask questions and be involved in the process
- Expediting the settling of your estate
- Preserving relationships

You don't have to discuss specific assets or disclose inheritances because that isn't the purpose of these meetings. Your estate will change over the years, and it may look very different when you pass away than when you created your plan.

While these may be emotional meetings, the effort to bring together this group is well worth your time. It will help those you leave behind to trust they are following your wishes and feel better prepared to handle estate matters when you pass away.

WRITTEN LETTERS

Whether you meet with those designated to manage parts of your estate plan or not, providing a written letter of instruction (aka letter of intent or explanatory letter) can make a difficult job easier.

The information and messages you share in the letters will vary depending on each person's role in your life and plan.

Letter to Your Executor or Trustee

A personal representative or trustee's job is to manage and help settle your estate according to your will or trust. Examples of information they may benefit from include:

- Funeral and burial preferences and information
- List of your assets or trust property and their location
- Insurance company information, policies that are in effect, and beneficiaries
- How to compensate a guardian caring for your minor children
- Contact information for creditors
- Names of beneficiaries on financial accounts
- Location of all your essential papers and how to access them
- Information about the future care of your pet(s)
- The why behind specific gift decisions
- Expectations on how beneficiaries should manage a shared property

Letter to Guardians of Minor Children

One of the most emotional letters you'll write is to the guardians of your minor children. You might begin this letter by focusing on the guardian and sharing the reasons you chose them to care for your child. This could include them having a strong bond with your child, sharing a similar parenting style, having similar values as yours, and more. You can also express your appreciation for everything they'll do for your child through the years.

You can then switch the focus of the letter to your child. Provide the guardian with identifying information, including your child's full legal name and Social Security number, and consider attaching a copy of an original birth certificate. Make sure to share the contact information for your child's physician, dentist, and other healthcare providers.

Then, provide information to help the guardian better understand your child's social, emotional, academic, and physical needs. Here are examples of some details you may include in your letter:

- Your family history and specific information on the child's relatives
- History of your child's milestones
- Medical conditions and prescriptions
- Educational experiences and academic interests
- Personality traits, disposition, behavior management
- Preferred social activities and friends
- Favorite books, toys, foods, games, shows
- Hobbies, sports, clubs, musical interests
- Dislikes and fears
- Religious preferences

You can also share the hopes and dreams you have for them, along with any concerns you may have about their future.

These are examples of instruction letters you can leave for loved ones along with your estate planning documents. You may decide to write letters to your POAs to help them with difficult decisions they may have to make as well. Some people also choose to leave a final note with touching memories and messages for family members and friends. Also, don't forget to update your letters when you review your estate plan.

DOCUMENT STORAGE AND ACCESSIBILITY

Keeping Your Plan Safe and Accessible

Once you create estate planning documents, you need to decide where to store them and who should have access to the information. The blanket advice you'll hear is to keep your paperwork in a safe and readily accessible location.

But keep in mind that each part of your plan serves a different purpose, so safe and accessible may look different depending on the form. Personal circumstances will impact some decisions about where to store documents, who to share them with, and when.

STORAGE AND ACCESS CONSIDERATIONS

You may decide to keep your originals in a waterproof and fireproof safe and keep a copy of them in a binder on a shelf for easy access. Some people choose to store them in a safe deposit box at a local bank. Just make sure someone you trust can get into the safe or safe deposit box if you become incapacitated or pass away.

A digital backup of your paperwork is another option. You can scan hard copies and save digital copies onto a thumb drive and secure it in your safe or safe deposit box. Cloud storage is available, but privacy and security might be a concern. You may need to give loved ones passwords to access those digital accounts too.

Another possibility is storing your original signed paperwork at your attorney's office. If you're considering this choice, discuss it with your lawyer as you work on your estate plan.

Keep in mind that if someone has to act on your behalf, they may need signed original forms instead of a copy. And remember to keep a list of everyone you provide with estate planning documents.

Whenever you amend, revoke, or create a new form to replace an old version, collect and destroy the originals, so there isn't any confusion.

Next we'll look at some essential estate planning documents and discuss which storage options you might consider, along with who needs access to them and when, and how to provide that information.

Advance Healthcare Directive

You create a durable power of attorney for healthcare and a living will to protect yourself. But if you end up hospitalized and are incapacitated, it's crucial agents can quickly access this paperwork. Without them, your agent might not be allowed to make medical decisions for you. Medical staff may not follow your end-of-life healthcare preferences either.

You can keep the original forms in your chosen safe location. And you might consider putting the name and contact numbers of your healthcare agents and the place of your paperwork on a card in your wallet.

Share the originals' location with your healthcare agent and alternate agents in case they need to produce them. But they should have copies to keep in their files too. Provide copies of both forms to your physician and the local hospital also, so they become a part of your medical records.

Financial Power of Attorney

Your financial POA gives your agent the ability to manage your finances within the scope of the agreement. When you execute the document, you may choose to sign several original copies. Safely store all the original copies you don't distribute to others with other estate planning paperwork.

If your agent is to act on your behalf immediately, give them an original copy of your paperwork. Depending on your circumstances, you may also decide to provide an alternate agent a copy too. You may choose to hold off on sharing a financial POA if your agent won't act until you become incapacitated.

Financial institutions generally require original signed power of attorney forms, and some even have their own POA forms. Check with your lender to understand their process and requirements.

Living Trust

Securely store trust paperwork with your other estate planning documents. And because you're likely the trustee and beneficiary of your living trust, it doesn't make sense to share it with others in most cases. As the trustee, you'll likely need a copy of your trust to transfer certain types of property into it.

Your designated replacement trustee should know where to locate and access the document. This will allow them to follow the directions you've left behind about distributing trust assets to your beneficiaries.

If you have minor children, you should talk with your attorney about who should get a copy of your trust paperwork. They may suggest that the custodian of the trust assets your children will inherit should have a copy of the trust document to prove their authority to manage the property.

Last Will and Testament

After drafting your will, you should safely store the original with other estate planning papers. Since it has no power during your lifetime and you may decide to amend it or create a new one, you may choose to keep your will private. But keep in mind that your representative should know the location of your original will and how to access it because it's usually required to start probate proceedings.

Should Your Attorney Store Your Will?

When you leave your original will with your attorney, your executor may feel obligated to retain them to work through probate and the settling of your estate. This may be your preference, but consider a different option for storing your will if you have any reservations about their fees or performance.

It may make sense to give the original copy of your will to your representative to keep it safe in some circumstances. But leaving it with your attorney may be an option too. Even if you don't want your attorney to store the original, they'll likely keep a digital copy of your will for some time.

WHEN TO CHANGE YOUR PLAN

Don't Just Leave It in a Drawer

If you've completed your estate plan—congratulations! The majority of American adults still don't have even the most basic estate planning elements done. But remember what we said at the beginning of this book: Estate planning is a process, and it doesn't end at the signing of some papers.

Instead, the passing of time and changes in your life should prompt you to review your plan and may require you to consult with an estate planning attorney or financial professionals.

REVIEWING YOUR PLAN

Keeping your plan up to date helps to make sure you're meeting estate planning goals throughout your lifetime. It also helps ensure your wishes will be followed and loved ones protected after you pass away. If you put your estate plan aside and fail to review it regularly or update it when needed, unintended consequences might occur.

It's a good idea to do a quick annual review of your plan and take a more in-depth look every few years and always when a significant life event occurs.

Here are some ideas for what to include in these reviews:

- **Insurance planning.** Look at your insurance policies and increase coverage or buy new policies as needed. Cancel existing insurance if it's no longer necessary. Review designated and contingent beneficiaries and make required updates.

- **Tax planning.** Review changes to the tax code to make sure you're taking advantage of tax credits and increases to annual IRA, 401(k), or HSA contribution amounts you're eligible for. Make a plan to bunch expenses and charitable donations to itemize deductions, if possible.
- **Financial planning.** Update your net worth and review your spending, saving, and investing. Can you increase contributions to your tax-advantaged savings accounts, open new ones, or start a 529 Plan for a new child or grandchild?
- **Estate planning.** Go over all your estate planning tools—will, POAs, advance directives, trusts—at least every three to five years. This will help you identify any modifications you might need. Remember, you can only make changes when you're legally competent. If you procrastinate and are later found mentally incapacitated due to an illness or injury, you can't change your estate plan.

Also, look through your emergency binder, update information, and make any necessary adjustments to your business's emergency and succession plans.

When to Update Estate Plan Documents

The following significant life changes usually require you to add or remove individuals from certain forms and revise beneficiaries on others.

Marriage/Remarriage

When you say, "I do," it's time to update much of your estate plan. A new spouse may become your designated agent on POA forms, and you'll want to add them to your will or trust as a beneficiary. Also, review beneficiary designations on life insurance policies, bank accounts, investment accounts, and retirement accounts. This helps prevent assets from going to someone other than your spouse. If you have children from a previous relationship, make sure to include them, so they aren't accidentally disinherited when you die.

Domestic Partnership

If you register a domestic partnership, update POAs if you want your partner to make healthcare decisions or manage your finances in case of your incapacitation. You'll also need to add them to your will or trust to be sure your wishes are followed and your partner is protected. If you fail to do so, they might not receive anything when you pass away.

Divorce

Visit your estate planning attorney to modify your paperwork if your marriage is ending. Remove your former spouse as a beneficiary of your will, trust, life insurance policy, retirement accounts, and other financial accounts. Taking this step can keep your ex-spouse from receiving assets you intend to go to others.

Birth of Children

When you have a new child, either through birth or adoption, add your child to your estate plan. In your will, make sure to name a guardian to care for them if you die before they become adults. (Revisit your choice for a guardian regularly to make sure they are still the person you want for this role.)

If you have children from a prior relationship, address both sets of children in your estate plan. Similarly, include any stepchildren or grandchildren you'd like to receive assets from your estate.

Can You Now Disinherit an Heir?

If something happens that makes you want to disinherit a child, address this in your estate plan. Talk to an estate planning attorney to ensure this type of change complies with your state's inheritance laws.

Serious Illness or Injury

If a family member gets severely injured or suffers from a serious illness, revisit your POAs, will, or trust to make updates and protect yourself and the interests of loved ones.

Death

If a beneficiary listed in your estate plan passes away, it's crucial to make updates. Review all your paperwork and determine whether changes are necessary. This includes revisiting beneficiary designations on life insurance policies, retirement accounts, and other financial accounts to update them. If the deceased is a beneficiary of your will or trust, decide how to revise your current beneficiaries' asset distribution.

Selling Assets

If you sell a property you've gifted to a beneficiary in your will or trust, make sure to consider the impact of the sale on that beneficiary's inheritance.

Changes in Tax Laws

You'll need to pay attention to tax laws because they frequently change. Similarly, if you relocate, you'll want to be sure your estate planning paperwork reflects the laws of your new location.

If you have a large estate or have accumulated substantial wealth since your last estate plan update, sit down with an attorney to ensure your plan provides you and your family with the most generous tax savings.

Other Things to Consider

These situations should also prompt you to revise your plan:

- Your minor children become adults
- You want to update trust beneficiaries
- You want to add or remove an executor or successor trustee
- You want to change the authority granted under a power of attorney
- You want to change your living will
- You open a business and need to plan for succession
- You purchase property in other states
- You start retirement
- A substantial financial change occurs

Regularly reviewing your plan, making adjustments, and updating forms after significant life changes can ensure everything accurately reflects your desires and current laws. If a review of your estate plan reveals any issues, address them promptly so others can follow your wishes.

INDEX

ABOUT THE AUTHORS

Vicki Cook is the cofounder of *Women Who Money* and *Women's Money Talk*, and the founder and blogger behind *Make Smarter Decisions*. She's been a regular contributor to *GOBankingRates*, *Medi-Share*, and a variety of personal finance sites around the web. She enjoys writing about real estate investing, financial independence, career decisions, and travel.

Vicki holds a doctoral degree in educational leadership from the University of Rochester. She's been a high school science teacher, a school administrator, and a college professor in her thirty-two-year career as an educator. She's also been a landlord for twenty-five years. Vicki left full-time employment after achieving financial independence and is now pursuing passion projects.

Amy Blacklock is the cofounder of *Women Who Money* and *Women's Money Talk*, and the founder and blogger behind the award-winning site *Life Zemplified*. She's been a frequent contributor to *GOBankingRates*, *WealthFit*, *Medi-Share*, and to a variety of personal finance sites around the web. She enjoys writing about mindful spending and saving, retirement planning, and financial independence.

Amy holds a bachelor's degree in integrative studies with a minor in human resource development from Oakland University. She's an entrepreneur at heart, previously owning two businesses and holding positions in accounting, human resources, and project management within the automotive industry. She now devotes her time to family and passion projects to help others improve their health and wealth.